Mossad

Legacy of Israel's National Intelligence Agency

(The Untold Stories of Israel's Most Effective Secret Service)

Candido Rolfson

Published By **Zoe Lawson**

Candido Rolfson

All Rights Reserved

Mossad: Legacy of Israel's National Intelligence Agency (The Untold Stories of Israel's Most Effective Secret Service)

ISBN 978-1-77485-913-1

No part of this guidebook shall be reproduced in any form without permission in writing from the publisher except in the case of brief quotations embodied in critical articles or reviews.

Legal & Disclaimer

The information contained in this ebook is not designed to replace or take the place of any form of medicine or professional medical advice. The information in this ebook has been provided for educational & entertainment purposes only.

The information contained in this book has been compiled from sources deemed reliable, and it is accurate to the best of the Author's knowledge; however, the Author cannot guarantee its accuracy and validity and cannot be held liable for any errors or omissions. Changes are periodically made to this book. You must consult your doctor or get professional medical advice before using any of the suggested remedies, techniques, or information in this book.

Upon using the information contained in this book, you agree to hold harmless the Author from and against any damages, costs, and expenses, including any legal fees potentially resulting from the application of any of the information provided by this guide. This disclaimer applies to any damages or injury caused by the use and application, whether directly or indirectly, of any advice or information presented, whether for breach of contract, tort, negligence, personal injury, criminal intent, or under any other cause of action.

You agree to accept all risks of using the information presented inside this book. You need to consult a professional medical practitioner in order to ensure you are both able and healthy enough to participate in this program.

TABLE OF CONTENTS

Introduction 1

Chapter 1: Operation Garibaldi 2

Chapter 2: A Different Nazi Fugitive 11

Chapter 3: Black September Organization Black September Organization 25

Chapter 4: The Things The Mossad Did Not Know About Salameh 38

Chapter 5: Egyptian Nuclear Scientists ... 49

Chapter 6: Mordechai Vanunu 58

Chapter 7: The Rise Of The Mossad 80

Chapter 8: The Six-Day War 148

Chapter 9: Wrath Of God 170

Introduction

The Mossad is an intelligence organization that is responsible for collecting intelligence as well as covert operations, counterterrorism as well as in bringing Jews to Israel and securing Jewish communities. It is also endorsed by State of Israel, that is, it is authorized to kill. Some have called the agency the "killer machine" and a lot of its activities make it the subject of a death sentence. It collects information and teams of people who carry out assassinations. Although some of these assassinations are to be heroic, others are controversial, while others aren't. A lot of these operations are secret, but there's a vast quantity of information accessible to the general public. The book guides the reader through the various assassinations and operations of the Mossad by highlighting its achievements as well as its failings.

I hope you enjoy it!

Chapter 1: Operation Garibaldi

"If you don't stop you'll be shot." is the message that the Mossad team told their team after being captured by Nazi exile Adolf Eichmann, one of the most important figures of the Holocaust. "The "head butcher" Isser Harel, the director at the time, was referring to Eichmann as. The capturing, dubbed Operation Garibaldi, was the Mossad's debut high-profile case.

Adolf Eichmann was appointed to the Jewish section of the security service from the Shutzstaffel in 1934, a year following Adolf Hitler took office. The Shutzstaffel was headed by Eichmann who came up with the concept of deporting Jews to ghettos. this deportation later became the extermination of Jews. Eichmann also wrote the address delivered by the senior Nazi official Reinhard Heydrich. In terms of the law He was a major enemy of the Jews.

"This dark period within the story of the Jewish people terrified me like a dream which was untrue to the real world. The events went beyond the boundaries of savage crime, blatant violence, and eternal hatred that nobody could comprehend the significance of it," Harel wrote in his memoir about the incident.

The Jews were forever in the grip of the Nazis However, it was evident that on white paper Eichmann and many others were largely lost to history. He was never found and, after a few years post-Holocaust , nobody was searching. It was impossible to locate him in the months following May 1945, when his escape from the Nuremberg trials as well as his capture by the "Nokhim," (Avengers) who enslaved thousands of SS men.

Eichmann was within Europe up to 1950 but without having contact or communication with his relatives. He was able to escape to Argentina along with two other ex- SS men, operating under the name Ricardo Klement, and lived in San Fernando, Tucuman, and later Buenos Aires, working various tasks.

Although he took care to eliminate any evidence of his previous self but his sons weren't. Evidently, they utilized their family name without hesitation and one even told an Argentinian Jewish girl, without aware that she was Jewish and about his father's role in the killing of Jews throughout Europe.

Eichmann had seemingly disappeared, until 1957. Walter Eytan, Director-General of the Ministry of Foreign Affiars called Harel and set up for an emergency meeting. A letter sent by the Dr. Shinar, head of the Reparations Mission in West Germany informed him to Harel that Adolf Eichmann was alive and his address was known. The information was provided by the Dr. Fritz Bauer, Public Prosecutor for the Province of Hesse in West Germany who was dedicated to finding and bringing Nazi War Criminals and their families to justice. He desired to see Eichmann arrested and tried, however the prosecutor was not sure how they could count on the German justice system of the embassy staff located in Buenos Aires. He turned to Shinar and the information was given to Harel.

They had received information about Eichmann previously, but they were unsuccessful in locating any trace of his. But this time Harel was unusually optimistic. He received the approval of Ben Gurion, the prime minister at the time, and began his mission.

Harel had a plan to take down Eichmann and have him put on for trial in Israel. Harel carefully selected a group of talented and reliable people who had also lost the majority or all of their families to Nazi camps. They were aware of what this could affect people of the Jewish people. Rafi Eitan was the commander of the team to capture. The team was manned by someone for everything logistics key copying, forging concealing places, performing medical services, as well as doing makeup for faces.

When they arrived in Argentina they had plans for everything. They were dressed as tourists. Even equipment used to copy was disguised as art tools. Nobody knew who they really were. The group would only speak with Harel in the crowded coffee shops and eateries. They used a variety of vehicles as well as apartments and homes.

The group followed Bauer's tip towards Garibaldi Street in the San Fernando area from Buenos Aires. They also learned that Eichmann lived as Ricardo Klement, and they kept a close eye on the house. The Klement family matched the Eichmann family's description, but at a time when photos weren't clear and fingerprints inaccessible as well, the Mossad team had no proof that he was the Nazi they were after.

One day, Klement was picked up from the bus carrying flowers and opened the door of his home. There, his children and wife were dressed in nice clothes. They were clearly celebrating. The date was March 21st in 1960. the 21st of March marked Eichmann's second wedding anniversary. It was no coincidence, but it proved the information they required. They were now able to devise an escape plan Eichmann.

Harel was in Argentina to supervise the operation. They were planning to capture Eichmann and then fly him away using fake documents. Everybody in Mossad was carrying fake documents, as well as from across the globe. They had connections to planes as well as visas, health certificates and characters references...the everything. They didn't have to raise suspicions with those in the Argentinian government. Israel could be breaking Argentinian sovereignty by abducting and capturing Eichmann and it did not aid that Argentina was filled with Nazi sympathizers. The reason for the flight into

Buenos Aires was Argentina's 150th anniversary celebrations.

The action on May 11th started. Two Mossad agents parked 30 yards away from one another in Klement's street around 7:35 p.m just five minutes prior to when the normal time of return from work. Since he was late this particular day and the Mossad team started to express doubts about the operation but by 8:05 he had finally appeared. He walked up to one of the vehicles, in which Zvi Malhin was. Malhin knew Klement could have carried an arsenal, but managed to get Klement down. They dragged Klement into the car which was gagged. He had his feet and hands tied and required to wear glasses that blocked his vision. He was silent and did not refuse. He remained still and wasn't injured.

They brought Eichmann to a secure home where they removed his clothes, put on pajamas for him, and then tied Eichmann's leg on a bedframe similar to a scene from the film. They screened him for poison , so that it wouldn't be a suicide risk. He did not try too difficult to conceal his identity. Then did he agree to cooperate, in terror of Mossad team. He was locked inside the cell for nearly a week while they planned out ways to escape Argentina. The family of Eichmann contacted hospitals, clinics and even their family members but did not notify authorities until after.

The team arranged a flight to fly on May 20th. A few days prior, they took one of their employees to an area hospital to claim that the brain had been damaged. The morning of May 20 the results showed that he was healthy enough to fly back to Israel. They obtained the certificate and put Eichmann's photo and name in the application. They injected him with drugs when they took him to the plane. They all wore uniforms for the flight crew. Once again, Eichmann made it easy for the crew and cooperated completely. Two guys accompanied Eichmann to the plane two on each side to support him, and had no problems.

On the 15th of December, the year 1961 Eichmann was tried before the Jewish community in Jerusalem in a bulletproof glass box. There, forgotten memories were revealed for many Jews. Eichmann attempted to claim that the fact that he was just following instructions, but the extent of his deeds was revealed. He was seeking understanding and compassion and he didn't get either. There was no mercy or understanding. Holocaust was a major issue that affected all people, and the trial was intended to be thorough and informative. The trial focused on the Holocaust as well as the Jews and the Jews, which was distinct than the Nuremberg trials as well as other camps, which focused on war criminals and criminals. It was a more intimate event for the Jewish citizens of Israel. On May 31, 1962, Eichmann was hanged.

Operation Garibaldi was a humbling mission for Jewish people all over the world and transformed Israel. It was able to bring the war criminals to justice. It was personal to each person on the team, since they all lost families or friends in the hands of Nazis. They wanted to pay back the gruesome deaths of a lot of Jews. While the majority of people would want the same, a lot of people were of the opinion that going far into South America to chase down one individual was not the most efficient use of resources for the intelligence department. Eichmann was no an immediate menace to Jewish people, so it was known to everyone and others who were close in proximity to Israel could have presented the immediate threat. In fact, many Jewish people were skeptical of Garibaldi so it is possible to imagine what the people of the other countries considered. However, this particular operation led to a trial that many Jews would have believed was essential. Others had results which were more controversial but we'll talk about that later.

Chapter 2: A Different Nazi Fugitive

Mossad pursued Justice for Jewish people. Herberts Cukurs, aka the "Butcher of Riga," was another Nazi member who was not brought to for trial following the Holocaust. He was an airman and was involved with the massive killing of Latvian Jews.

On the 6th of March, 1965 Uruguayan officers Alejandro Otero was received a letter from an anonymous source with the name "We Can't Forget," of the news that Shangrila, Uruguay, Cukurs was dead. The letter contained a contact number to the place where Otero was able to find Cukurs dead and bloody. Cukurs was beat and killed on the head. The body was next to it was an excerpt from the pleadings of an accused British accused in the Nuremberg trials, which the media claimed was evidence of the mass killing of Jews. Even though Mossad did not publicly come out regarding its involvement right away the murder, many believed they were the ones responsible.

"The government of Israel had decided to remove the most prominent Nazi War criminals. This was a particular method of elimination that was selective and efficient.

The most famous one included Herberts Cukurs who had committed horrible crime on Latvian Jews and had escaped the persecution of his allies."

This is the story Meir Amit, Mossad Chief in the 1960s and '60s, wrote in the preface to an article published in Keter Publishing Company. Israeli Keter publishing house. The book, entitled The Experiment of the hangman of Riga described the execution in details. The book was not published until 1997. Isser Harel was not able to reveal Mossad's involvement in executions until 1985, a sign of secrecy within the organization as well as its operation of covert tactics. The book was intended to influence debate on the limitations on Nazi crimes, yet certain people believed it was an "product of the department of 'disinformation..'"

When he spoke to Yitzhak, Yedioth Aharonoth explained how he was involved in the sting operation. He disguised himself in the disguise of an Austrian, Anton, and became friends with Cukurs who had ideas for business on tourism and Brazil. They had a great time together. They traveled extensively and Anton even got to meet Cukurs his family.

There were numerous occasions that Anton and Cukurs to take on one another in Brazil as well as other cities they made trips, but the execution didn't take place until the following day within Montevido, Uruguay. Based on the Mossad plan, the idea was to read the accusations against Cukurs before executing the accused, leaving a clear statement for all. Four men were responsible for the operation and they were armed with an assortment of cars, hotels, rental hotels passports, passports and other documentation scheduled for the duration period of time they were in.

Anton said he was using this house located in Montevido as an office for a while when he took Cukurs to the house. When the two of them were inside the house, the Mossad team took off after Cukurs and he fought back and eventually killed Cukurs. The next day, they handed over the police a tip regarding the location of the body.

Mossad has claimed that he was planning to murder The Nazi who were in Uruguay rather than Brazil due to the fact that Brazil was a country with death penalties, which meant there could be the possibility of the group being arrested. They had hoped to have the execution be a public declaration in addition. Others question the real motive of the execution. Officer Otero was able to investigate the murder and discovered evidence that suggested the group was trying to abduct Cukurs but not to take him to the grave. One of the items he observed was that the body was kept in a container with metal buckles and air holes to prevent the chest from opening from the inside. This suggested they intended to bring Cukurs to the hospital alive.

Cukurs is likely to have been executed regardless of whether in Uruguay or Israel like Eichmann was. The debate is about the issue of whether the motive to carry out the task was different and the intention was different, then Mossad did not disclose the truth in their disclosures to the public decades later. This erodes the confidence of the public. After a number of other Mossad missions, they are not a secret, the public is aware that the Mossad is full of secrets. And when Cukurs was and Eichmann were wanted as war criminals (and naturally, they were retribution) however, the Mossad executes a variety of other activities that aren't to everyone's advantage.

The other thing that is controversial about this particular operation is the evidence in support of Cukurs that is explained within The Execution of the Hangman of Riga. Margers Vestermanis, the head in Riga's Jewish museum located in Riga and a former slave laborer of the Nazis The book is "a complete sham." He has doubts about some of the quotations used as proof. He claims his belief that Cukurs is a member of the anti-Semitic wing of Perkonkrust is not proof enough.

Cukurs had also been a known participant in the Arajs known as a notorious murder unit. While he was an "chauffeur and right handman to Viktor Arajs, the head of the execution squad," there was some controversy over how personal his involvement was in the executions.

Some might say that Cukurs was rewarded for his work However, just as with Operation Garibaldi, the mission required a large amount of resources. The entire process of obtaining fake documents, communications homes, transportation, the list is endless -

could have cost huge amounts of time and money. Therefore, if Cukurs played a part in the massacre hundreds of Jews was not as significant as some believed, then many might not agree with the attention given to his execution particularly because he no longer posed an issue for the Jewish communities. Although Cukurs' operation was successful, some think it was revenge that Israel desired.

Background information on the Mossad

"For our country, which since its beginning is under attack by its adversaries. Intelligence is the first line of defense...we need to learn to be aware of the dangers within us."

Mossad's principal instruction, which was given in 1951 by David Ben Gurion, the Premier Minister in 1951.

The 1st of April 1951 Gurion created Mossad in order to take over the Central Institute for Coordination, which was created to enhance coordination between Shabak, AMAN, and the political department that comprised the Foreign Office in 1949. It was established immediately following the creation of the State of Israel. In the past it was believed that the name of the person who directed Mossad was classified as a secret of the state up until the month of March, in which the state announced that Major General Danny Yatom as the replacement for Shabtai Shavit who had resigned at the beginning of the year. The late 1980s saw the Mossad staff was believed to be between 1,500 and 2,200, and later 1,200.

Mossad includes eight department. The Collections Department is the largest and has responsibility for spying operations.

The Political Action and Liaison Department is responsible for political activities with other nations. Israel isn't able to establish normal diplomatic relations with, as well as foreign intelligence agencies.

The Special Operations Division, or Metsada is responsible for extremely sensitive assassination, sabotage paramilitary, as well as psychological warfare projects.

LAP (Lohamah Psichlogit) Department is responsible for propaganda, psychological warfare and deceit operations.

Research Department is responsible for daily reports and summary documents. It is comprised of 15 geographically specific sections scattered across the world.

The details of these other divisions, as others of Mossad are hazy. According to the website, intelligence gathering is always in the interest of the State and is monitored within the EEI The EEI, which stands for the Essential Elements of Information, via the use of HUMINT (human intelligence) and SIGINT (signals intelligence). "The routine operation is not disclosed to the public for reason that is understandable." The extent of actual activities carried out by Mossad isn't known as a result of the fact that numerous details of well-known operations are disclosed to the public by Mossad agents, one could say that they are propaganda. But, there are some that aren't as controversial, as you'll find out. The next time we'll examine the Mossad's part in the downfall of and shaming the Soviet Union.

Nikita Khrushchev's Speech Capture

A few years later, after Josef Stalin died, Nikita Khrushchev decried Stalin in a speech addressed to Communist party members. He detailed the crimes of the dictator in the speech, stating that "far from God, Stalin was satanic." The speech was never meant for publication. The speech was read by the local secretaries of the party, who were even required to return the speech within 36 hours.

Soviet sources have even claimed that some of the delegate suffered heart attacks or even committed suicide after hearing the speech since the information was unsettling and painful to contemplate.

John Rettie explains how his Russian contact Kostya Orlov called him to set up an appointment for a meeting on March 26, 1956. Orlov stated that the party across all of the Soviet Union had heard of the speech during special gatherings, and members were shocked. Stalin was once thought of as to be a hero of the nation, so knowing about his crimes was devastating to those who used to look at him as a leader as well as hero.

Rettie wasn't sure of what she believed at the time, because very few people were aware of or believed that Stalin was a dictator in the moment, however Orlov was a reliable source to his superiors. Orlov also made the claim in a bid to break the restriction on speech. Rettie and his reporter from Moscow, Sidney Weiland, believed Orlov. Rettie took notes and dictated the notes to a news editor in London and made sure that his identity was hidden from the report.

The full text of Khrushchev's speech was first published for the first times in Observer along with The New York times. William Taubman explains in his biography of Khrushchev that the text was leaked to Poland and Poland, in which Moscow had provided copies for distribution to Polish party. It appears that printers printed thousands extra copies that they weren't permitted to print. One was seized by the Mossad. The Mossad handed it over on to CIA. The CIA transferred it on to newspaper the New York times and Edward Crankshaw The editor of the Observer's Kremlinologist.

A lot of lives were affected once the speech went widely known. The former Gulag prisoner Marina Okrugina, told The Guardian, "Finally, in 1956, only a couple of months after Khrushchev's speech I was completely rehabilitated. My life was transformed." The publication in the United States of the speech proved what many were skeptical of. The speech exposed shocking truths to the world in addition to causing embarrassment for the USSR.

The Blue Bird - Operation Diamond

"Get me a Mig-21," IAF commander Ezer Weizman told Meir Amit, the head of Mossad at the time, 1965. A film created by the Israel Intelligence Heritage and Commemoration Center provided some information about Operation Diamond, a mission to secure the aircraft. It was among the most advanced aircraft used by Arab forces at the time. The Mossad was aware that Egypt owned 34 versions of these types of aircraft, Syria had 18, and Iraq had 10.

Within Iraq, Mossad was connected to Yosef Shemesh Yosef Shemesh, who was a Jewish businessman, who was involved with the daughter-in-law of Redfa who was who was an Iraqi Air Force pilot. Redfa was unhappy with the fact that he was not able to get an increase within the Iraqi army due to his Christian heritage. Shemesh connected him with the Mossad through an agent who was female who convinced him to take him to Europe.

Redfa was able to meet the IAF pilot at Rome. They flew together to Israel and Redfa was on a plane together with an IAF Intelligence Chief at that time. The Premier of the government Levy Eshkol was informed of the plan about a month prior to the attack.

There were some obstacles in the course of the operation. Mossad agents traveled to Iraq to help the family of Redfa get out of Iraq However, Redfa did not inform them about the mission. his wife Betty is angry, and threatened call the Iraqi Embassy. Betty was eventually calmed and was taken to a safe place within Iraq.

Redfa piloted the Mig-21 on the Tuesday of August 16 in 1966. While he flew flying over Jordan the plane was spotted. Syria was contacted , but was assured by Jordan that the plane was part of Syria's air force. Syrian air force and allowed for the plane to fly with no doubt.

Redfa arrived safely, meeting the two Israeli Air Force Dassault Mirage III's, an aircraft built by the French Air Force and also exported to other nations. They took him to an landing in Hatzor. It appears that the Mig-21 had made it to the ground with none of the fuel remaining.

After spending a month in Israel The plane was transferred to the American Air Force for testing and for intelligence. In return, Israel got US-made Phantoms. In the wake of studies conducted regarding Mig-21 Mig-21, Israeli fighter jets were able of shooting down hundreds of Mig-21 aircraft from the rival forces. The US also gained from studying the Mig-21 plane.

Sources point out the importance that female Mossad personnel in this particular operation, along with other operations. Agents identified as Yael tells Times of Israel that there are some advantages women enjoy over men "A male who seeks to gain access into a restricted zone has a lower chance of getting in... If a woman is smiling, she has a better chance of being allowed in. happy woman is more likely of getting the job done." This Mossad have carefully selected a person they could track down to pilot the plane during the mission, Redfa, someone who might also be enticed by an attractive woman.

We observe that the Mossad uses innovative strategies for getting trust from allies and adversaries. For instance, in Cukurs, in Cukurs operations, "Anton" had to wait for months to gain Cukurs his trust but even then Cukurs was skeptical, and he kept his eyes on all times. It could be different had Mossad chose someone to befriend him even though she might not have lured him with business plans. The decisions made in the execution of the task show the cautious methods Mossad is required to employ for each task.

As you progress you'll find that the most precise operations are further back in time. The Mossad maintains its operations as a secret for many years, possibly to minimize the chance of retaliation from adversaries. The details are only provided by the agency its own personnel, which is understandable but we're not sure what extent the agents overplay their missions and the actions they take. They're probably as exciting and thrilling as we imagine, however there are some details the Mossad will not want the general public to learn.

Chapter 3: Black September Organization
Black September Organization

On the 5th of September in 1972 Arab terrorists broke into Olympic Village Apartments in Munich and planned to capture Israeli athletes. They first took 11 athletes hostage, then shot the coach of the wrestling team, Moshe Weinberger, in the head. The teammate David Marc Berger escaped, while Yossef Romanno tried but failed toescape, and then was killed. Within an hour the 2 Israeli players were murdered and nine were rescued. The remaining eight athletes could not be identified at the time of the incident two of them escaped and alerted authorities.

The terrorists wrote requests and dumped Weinberger's body onto the streets. They demanded for the freedom of the 234 Arab and German prisoners by Israel in Israel and West Germany, and three planes to escape including a plane to Cairo to visit prisoners who are to release from Israel.

Golda Meir, Israel's prime minister, has made it clear that Israel will not be negotiating with terrorists. German police negotiators were able extend three deadlines set by terrorists. They were however unable to gain support from Egypt's government. Egypt. Manfred Schreiber, the Munich Police Commissioner, decided that a rescue must be conducted to help the athletes.

Mossad chief Zwi Zamir traveled to Munich to seek permission from Israeli commandos to conduct the rescue of hostages, however the local officials of the state did not agree to the assistance, sadly. In the initial attempt to help by German Police an grenade was dropped by Fedayeen's gang into the helicopter carrying five Israeli athletes, and they died all. Following that the incident, another Fedayeen group member shot and killed the final four hostages of another helicopter. Zamir as well as the Israeli Government, naturally was shocked that the German Police did not cooperate with specially trained police officers.

The Palestinian Black September Organization took responsibility for the attack. They orchestrated 9 major terror attacks between 1970 and the beginning of 1972, before the attack in Munich.

Meir advised "Israel will not relinquish her fight against terrorist groups and will not excuse their collaborators from the responsibility of the terrorist acts." He came up with the new counterterrorism strategy. He along with General Aharon Yariv and Zamir convinced that the Israeli Cabinet to establish an "top secret counterterrorism group." Meir and Defense Minister Moshe Dayan were the chairmen of the group, "Committee-X," which was given by the Mossad the task of killing members of the BSO. BSO members.

The first attempt to assassinate BSO head Ali Hassan Salameh was a total failure, whereas many other attempts were successful. However, there was one attempt that was a total disaster.

The Lillehammer Affair

There were several teams of assassins to begin the mission and identify targets. The teams were separated so that they weren't aware of one another. Mike Harari, an intelligence officer in the Mossade was hoping to create an "interlocking information network that terrorist targets would not be able to escape." One team was run by the normal Mossad headquarters' procedures with regional resources and officers. Another team operated secretly and was backed by Mossad financially, yet denied having any association with the government. It was even required to follow an instruction list to get funds from secret accounts.

Salameh was the most wanted suspect for Mossad. After a year of looking and a year of searching, they received "confirmed" information that he was located in Lillehammer, Norway. Zamir was monitoring the deployments within Israel and Harari designed and manned the assassination squad.

On July 23, 1973, an team of assassins was on the lookout, and shot and killed the man that they believed was Salameh. The man was not Salameh but Ahmed Bouchiki, a Moroccan who was working as waiter. In essence, the Mossad had killed an innocent man, but the fatal Salameh was still around.

The police detained Dan Arbel and Marrianne Gladnikoff Two team members. Gladnikoff admitted to working with Israel's Government of Israel. There was an after-hours public trial for six of the Israeli Team members in which the details of the investigation were made public and five of them were found guilty of murdering the waiter. As per Dan Raviv, co-author of Every Spy a Prince, the five officers were sentenced between up to two and a-half years in prison. However, they were granted release by Norwegians within less than twenty-two months.

The punishment for team members is obviously controversial. Their inattention in identifying the target resulted into the innocent victim dying. Following this incident, the assassination teams became more cautious in the way they chose their targets and they achieved a significant number of successes.

The reason that the Lillehammer incident was so widely known and evidently a failure for the Mossad is most likely the only reason they chose to be extra cautious in the following actions that the task.

It is the Wrath of God

Another team of Harari's was under his pseudonym "Avner," which represented the leader of the team. The team consisted of five highly-trained individuals who had particular expertise in creating fake documents, obtaining vehicles, inventing explosives and many more, like in the other Mossad operations. Their goal was to separate them from leaders and "throw the entire organization into chaos" according to George Jonas' Vengeance (1984). They were totally secretive, and had even resigned their positions within the Mossad.

Although the paper trail leading of the Mossad was absent, they were issued official passports as well as intelligence from the Mossad agency. Harari handed them two fundamental guidelines. First, the group should be "imaginative and attack in innovative ways. In this way, terrorists would be aware that they were 'touched.'" The second was to "ensure that there is 100% recognition of the target prior to taking action." He also stressed that if innocent lives were sacrificed in the course of the operation, it would be classified as unsuccessful. This policy was a guarantee that something similar to that of the Lillehammer Affair would not happen in the future, and it could also be a nice face to present to the general public.

General Zamir offered an eleven-point list of prioritised targets. Some of these targets might have had access to security forces with guns however, others led more free-spirited lives, making them more attainable to hit. The group began to travel across Europe to establish connections and obtain accurate information about the locations of the target.

Avner identified a source that tried to get to the upper levels of the Baader Meinhof Red Army Faction. Avner offered the source with cash that the source didn't doubt, and he then set up an underground terrorist networks.

The first victim is Wael Zwaiter, a ringleader of terrorism across Europe who was based in Rome. The group traveled on their own to Ostia just a few miles away from Rome with Baretta .22 calibres as well as semi-automatic guns transported by an array of dealers.

Avner did know how to use his sources. His Baader-Meinhof Red Army Faction provided logistical support, staff to provide operational support, as well as surveillance on targets, without even being aware of the task at hand.

On the 16th of October, 1972, a group consisting of two vehicles made their way towards Zwaiter's apartment. The other was in charge of signalling the group once Zwaiter was seen coming out, which involved having a person exit the vehicle, then driving the female driver away. The couple's speed was increased by approximately a minute. Then it was followed by a blonde female rushing to the group, signalling that Zwaiter was on his own. The surveillance team was aware that Zwaiter was heading to a pub to make an appointment, since his phone service was shut off by the local company. Zwaiter then returned to the lobby, and the lighting was dim. A security guard asked him if he really was Wael Zwaiter. Zwaiter confirmedhis identity, and two agents fired fourteen rounds at the man. They removed all evidence off the scene.

The team was able to successfully take out one goal, but 10 targets remained at the top of the list.

Avner was presented to a brand fresh source of info "Louis," from "Le Group" in Paris. Louis's "Papa" developed an underground intelligence agency that was private to nongovernmental organizations. an official government entity, making it perfect for the covert group. They supplied information on the next attack, Mahmoud Hamshari, PLO participant who was also the coordinate of Munich. Munich incident.

At this point, a team member acted in the role of an Italian journalist, and asked for an interview with Hamshari to discuss an interview and that's how they identified Hamshari. On the 8th of December 1972 the "journalist" identified as Hamshari and identified him. and then the group executed an explosive attack, killing Hamshari.

Le Group provided support for the mission that was successful and targeted three other individuals listed on this list are Hussein Abd al-Chir and Dr. Basil al-Kubaisi, and Mohammed Boudia. They also assassinated Zaid Muchassi, who was not listed, but was replaced by Abad Al-Chir as Abad Al-Chir's replacement as PLO liaison with the KGB.

The decision to kill another person is a decision the team came up with, and it's logical. It also illustrates the spirit of initiative the team can take under certain circumstances. While in this instance, it appears to be a positive characteristic, some say when there are times when the Mossad has gotten out of hand.

Returning to the mission. On March 23, 1973 Harari called Avner and stated that he wanted the group to assist in an Mossad controlled military action in Beirut and also to kill three terrorists. Avner was uncertain about if he should go along, as Papa was not a supporter of the government's operations and he did not want to lose Le Group resources. Avner Harari Harari came up with a method to make use of Le Group's resources through collaboration together with Mossad in Beirut however, they did not perform their actual task.

The following April, Israel commandos struck multiple targets in Beirut which killed Adwan, Najjer, Nasser and around 100 PLO Guerrillas. Najjer's wife as well as a neighbor were also killed (two innocent victims).

In the latter part of 1973 Avner discovered the Lillehammer Affair and realized Harari was using several teams to fight similar PLO terrorists.

The public will be curious about which other teams were, as well as the other operations that took place. It's possible that the Israeli film is mainly details of Mossad operations. Mossad operations. They talk about the failed operations that were open to the public, but don't highlight any of the failures which could cause alarm to the public.

The next January in 1974, the Avner's team was unsuccessful in obtaining Salameh again, and killed 3 Arabs who were combatants however, they were not listed included on the list. It is possible that this was well-known because, even though the unit failed to hit their targets however, they did get three persons that could have been considered to be enemy.

The group was in May of 1974 when the group attempted to find an information source for Salameh in London However, one of Avner's associates was murdered by a woman in the hotel room in which they were staying. The group decided to follow the woman regardless of what their original purpose was. Le Group had determined she was an assassin working for a private company. They identified her as a freelancer in Amsterdam and then killed her in a stern warning to Le Group's enemies.

On the 14th of September 1974, another person from the team was shot dead in Belgium. There were some members who were concerned about the possibility that Le Group may have betrayed them, however Avner didn't believe in that because there were numerous possibilities that Papa might have lied to them but didn't. Maybe he knew that they were backed through the state. However the situation, Harari ordered the team to resign from the mission. But, Avner and the team took their own decision trying again for Salameh. Following complications, they canceled the procedure, marking the closure to the Wrath of God.

The team killed 8 of the initial 11 PLO terrorists, as well as one PLO leader who wasn't listed, and this took around two years. The collateral damage included one KGB officer as well as four PLO security officers, one assassin who was hired by a freelancer, and two members of the team. The covert operations carried out together and technically, without the involvement of the involvement of the government or Mossad was a huge success. Every person who was killed was an enemy (besides two members of the team) and the two who were killed by Israel the commandos weren't. The team took great care to kill only the individuals they targeted and the operation in conjunction in conjunction with Israel resulted in the killing of a huge number of enemies, but also two people as collateral damage.

Because all the information was provided by the Mossad in its own way, we must consider the actual specifics about the mission. Did they want to emphasize the particular care they took when removing targets from the list, whereas the mission with Israeli commandos was less exact? We'll never know, but we could be sure to speculate.

Chapter 4: The Things the Mossad did not know about Salameh

Between the the Lillehammer Affair and the Mossad's last attempt at assassinating Salameh, Salameh had actually been an CIA asset. They had hoped to leverage his connections and status in PLO organisations to defend the US. Salameh didn't take any money however, he was believed to want to improve relations between Americans as well as Palestinians. The CIA has denied any connection to Salameh to Israel that was the right decision.

Mossad dispatched the operative Erika Chambers out to Beirut to search for Salameh from 1978. Chambers posed as "an exaggerated English spinster employed at a charitable organization that cared of Palestinian children." Chambers, along with other agents conducted surveillance on Salameh who was discovered to have was frequently moving between PLO headquarters and the home that his wife had with him and their two children, as well as the residence that his wife had a second.

The team rented a car and then parked it with explosives close to the route that Salameh used to travel on. The explosives were detonated and were able to kill Salameh and also killed nine other people.

This was the primary purpose of the mission, however it is very little discussed and is a lot more controversial. Regarding the laws in God's Wrath of God, this mission was a complete fail. The other nine victims would have been inadmissible.

"It was as if it was. It was like a flash and then a huge explosion. It was awe-inspiring. I've never experienced something like it before, and not just in Beirut. It was like all of Beirut was in flames. There were dead bodies burning cars, young bodies littering the streets." The incident was noted by Marc E. Vargo, the author of "The Mossad: Six Landmark Operations that were conducted by the Israeli Intelligence Agency".

We must ask ourselves why the team did not carry the execution with the diligence and precision they have prior to. It's possible that it was an even more desperate effort or the team tried to establish a precedent. However, it was done at the expense of other people who were not involved. Perhaps they were hoping that the story was able to spread across the globe, revealing those who are enemies of the Mossad that they would be hunted down and executed. This is not a mission Israel has highlighted in its successful operation, and we could only imagine how many there are in the vast number of dead.

It's the Next Beirut Bombing

In 1983 in 1983, The Islamic militant organization Hazbollah loaded the truck with explosives to carry out an attack on US Marine barracks in Beirut. More than 250 American military personnel were killed.

Victor Ostrovsky said the Mossad provided specific information about the attack, gathered from an informant. Director Nahum Admoni did not alert American intelligence.

"We aren't here to defend Americans. They're a huge nation. You can just send them normal info," Admoni told his men. When he said normal, Admoni was referring to information on the possibility of danger coming from Lebanon but the information was likely to be not taken into consideration.

Ostrovsky is an ex Mossad agent who speaks very disdainfully of the organization, claiming that it exhibits been characterized as having a "total indifference to the human race." His book has been even being banned in the major bookstores because of the Israeli government's intervention. Ostrovsky is the few insiders we have who openly disagrees with Mossad's tactics. Many of his stories are reliable because they contain a lot of specifics and details the Mossad would not like being exposed. We will look at some of his tales in a subsequent chapter.

Assassinating Leaders

Chief Zamir stated that the purpose in The Wrath of God operations was to undermine the PLO's structure in Europe by separating its leaders from terrorists who required them. The Mossad always claimed that it was intended to collect data to safeguard Israel from the dangers its adversaries could be capable of imposing upon the country.

The sources that explain the specifics in The Wrath of God are most likely biased towards the Mossad. Although it targeted terrorists that could have been killed by other nations and also wanted to get rid of, some of the missions are controversial.

While the group of Avner's definitely succeeded in eliminating terrorists, some might have believed that the goal of their mission wasn't really to harm the PLO however, but rather to take revenge for the massacre that occurred in Munich. The motive could be in comparison with those involved that were behind that of Eichmann as well as Cukurs assassinations, two operations which targeted enemies who caused the most tragic incidents that were devastating for Jewish people. But, Eichmann as well as Cukurs were no longer in operation, whereas the PLO was very active in operation, and the comparisons are not completely similar.

As per David Kimche, former senior Mossad official, a few Mossad employees believed then the idea that "an intelligence agency shouldn't be involved with liquidation." But the intelligence community decided that only killing the top leaders of terrorist groups could have a strategic impact.

For instance the assassination of Zuheir Mohsen, the head of the pro-Syrian As-Sa'iqa group was the catalyst for the organization to disintegrate following the assassination. This assassination was believed to be the work of the Mossad although some think different theories. The assassination took place on the 25th of July, 1979, in Cannes, France.

The Mossad's most widely known operations involve assassinations of top leaders, not mass assaults as the organization wants to be depicted. The Mossad is known for brutal murders of enemies of Israel. Yet its eight departments are the source of a significant number of other intelligence sources that are which isn't connected to murders. We will then get an insider's view of Victor Ostrovsky, whose book was banned from book shops.

A former Israeli Mossad agent.

"I was thrilled when was selected and given the opportunity to be part of what I believed to be the top team that is the Mossad," wrote Victor Ostrovsky in his book Through deceit.

"But the absurd ideas and self-centered pragmatism I saw in the Mossad together with this"team"'s greed, lust and complete disregard for the human race, inspired me to share this tale."

The book by Ostrovsky is not available in the major chains of bookstores but it is accessible on the internet at sites like Amazon. Ostrovsky reveals the facts from his perspective as a Mossad employee Mossad during four consecutive years. He believes that the Mossad is in a state of chaos and that it is even the Prime Minister, to whom directs the director is not in any way a real influence over the Mossad's actions.

For instance, he states that a lot of Palestinians who are illegally crossing across the border in order to enter Israel are detained by Israeli forces and are never heard from ever again. A few are taken for deportation to ABC research facilities, where they endure "indescribable terror, or biological, nuclear, or chemical war."

He also described Operation Trojan, where Mossad transmitted disinformation that was later accepted through both the US in the US and Britain. They set up the Trojan device, which was a communications device within the territory of the enemy. The Trojan would broadcast prerecorded digital transmissions that could be received by Americans as well as the British.

The night of February 17th Israeli missile vessels sailed across the Mediterranean, let four submarines as well as two speedboats get off within their territorial waters in Libya. The submarines headed towards shore, while the agents headed towards the interior with their Trojan device. They were intercepted by an armed Mossad soldier who was there already, and then they headed towards the city, and moved into an apartment just three blocks of the Bab al Azizia barracks known to be the headquarters of Qadhafi's regime. They brought the gadget up to the upper floor in the structure, and activated it, and returned towards the shore. The soldier was monitoring the unit inside their apartment during the next couple of weeks.

The Trojan transmitted messages during high communications traffic hours. They appeared as a lengthy series of terrorist instructions to Libyan embassies all over the world. The Americans began to view Libyans as active sponsors of terrorism. Libyans as active supporters of terror, while French as well as

Spanish were skeptical. The Mossad employed America's promises to take retaliation against the support of terrorists, and to lure them into a ploy. Their goal was to obtain an advanced nation to strike Libya.

They were successful. On April 14 1986 One hundred sixty American aircrafts dropped more than sixty tons of explosives on Libya. A deal to liberation of American hostages held in Lebanon was struck and forty Libyan civilians were killed as did an American pilot and his weapons officer were killed.

For the Mossad the mission was an absolute success. It doesn't show this intelligence organization in similar manner like other news stories. It portrayed deceit towards the Americans whom typically seek to cooperate with. It "by clever sleight of hands has pushed at the United States to do what was right." It revealed to that the world on which position it was on. US stood on during the conflict between Israel and Arabs.

This is an illustration of what Ostrovsky was calling self-centered pragmatics. This mission was a great instance of Mossad setting Israel over other nations. It's not the only example of the kind of information Israel wanted to keep from being exposed to the general public.

A top Israeli source claims the book is fake However, the book is an "wealth of information," according to David Ignatius, Wall Street journalist. "He didn't come up with it up."

"They are determined to ruin my reputation. However, the truth is that this week, two Israeli agents came to my door and gave me money, no amount at all, in the event that I did not decide to publish my book. If I were interested in money, shouldn't I be able to take this from them? I'm not concerned about money. I wrote this book to take on a runaway group. Mossad's activities are costing Israel friends and, greater than every other weapon. Israel is in need of allies," says Ostrovsky, in reaction against Israeli authorities who deny his involvement in Mossad.

We must be aware about the degree of bias Ostrovsky could be. The reasons behind his departure from the Mossad are not clear, but his assessment of the organization is portrayed quite nicely.

Chapter 5: Egyptian Nuclear Scientists

Doctor. Yahya Al-Mashad was an Egyptian nuclear scientist from Egypt. He was a member of his organization, the Egyptian Atomic Energy Authority, and then travelled to Iraq and was the director of his role in the Iraqi Nuclear Program. He also oversees the nuclear cooperation agreement between Iraq and France.

Israel has sabotaged this program during the 80s. At the time, it was later believed that Mossad was behind the assassination attempt on Al-Mashad during the 1980s in Paris.

Many believe Al-Mashad wasn't the only, nor was he the only Egyptian Nuclear scientist to be killed by the Mossad and, as of today, we can all agree that the Mossad will do everything to defeat its enemies even if doing this by indirect means. Scientists aren't terrorists or enemies However, if they assist those in need, then they're targets of the Mossad.

A mysterious death that took place some time ago was the death of Dr. Ali Moustafa Mosharafa Pasha who published numerous documents and books and was awarded numerous achievements and distinctions. He was a researcher of Maxwell's equations as well as special relativity along with Albert Einstein, and was particularly interested in the work from Arab scientists. He also made many translations of his work into Arabic and Arabic, which would have been a mistake in the event that he didn't wish to be subject to the ire of Israel.

He was opposed to the use of science to cause destruction and war, but it seems that this wasn't enough to satisfy the Mossad. On January 15 in 1950, the scientist was murdered and it was believed that the Mossad was the culprit. A Islamic site lists him as one of the Arab scientists who were killed through Israeli Secret Services.

"I am shocked to learn that Mosharafa is gone, but the man is still alive thanks to his studies. We need his skills, it's an enormous loss. He was genius. I was a follower of his studies in the field of atomic energy. He is among the top scientists in the field of physics." is the quote from Einstein declared about his death.

The period of time between the death of Mosharafa and Al-Mashad is a sign of the continuing efforts by Israel to stop the advancement of nuclear technology to the Arabs.

Sameera Moussa was a physicist who was determined to make medical usage of nuclear technology accessible to everyone. She was the organizer of her Atomic Energy for Peace conference and was a believer that she was a part of "Atoms for Peace." She declared, "I'll make nuclear treatment affordable and accessible than aspirin."

On the 5th of August, 1952, she travelled to America and was then invited to go on a trip. While on the way the car fell 40 feet high and killed her instantly. The driver of the vehicle was also missing Many believe that Mossad was responsible. Mossad was also the culprit in the accident.

Many different deaths of Egyptian scientists are also attributed to the Mossad but nothing reliable has been proven.

The Nazi who was a part of Mossad

It wasn't just Egyptian scientists that the Mossad took aim at, however. Based upon interviews with members of the Mossad, German scientist Heinz Krug was executed in an Israeli method to make it harder for German scientists who worked for Egypt.

The most surprising aspect of this operation, however it was it was that the Mossad agent, Otto Skorzeny, who killed Krug was a former lieutenant colonel of the Waffen-SS and was believed to be was one of Hitler's "favorites". Skorzeny received an honorary medal, known as that of the Knight's Cross of the Iron Cross for leading the mission that saved Benito Mussolini.

After his death, Krug as well as others Germans employed in Egypt's rocket-building industry received threats informing them to stop this Egyptian program. In Egypt they were mailed letters bombs.

Krug was asked to go to Wernher Von Braun, one the founders of NASA in America however, he decided to join the scientists of the Peenemunde group in Egypt and establish the Arab programme for missiles. The Israelis believed that Israel was a potential attack target since there were a lot of Holocaust survivors living there and so they targeted the scientists who were part of the program.

The scientists realized that the threats in the notes and phone calls were made by Israelis and, following the time that Eichmann was kidnapped in the year 1960 they believed that the Mossad could be looking for Krug as well. Krug was a fan of Skorzeny, and called Skorzeny to seek help however, after they drove off together to someplace "safe," Krug was murdered and shot. Three Israelis put acid on his body , and later buried the remains of his body.

Skorzeny was Mossad's shady agent. He was used to gain as close possible to Nazis. They were required to make the alliance of someone who they would normally would have killed and this was difficult to accept for many. The Israelis were convinced that the man, just like Eichmann and Cukurs were involved in the killing of Jews. He was even featured as Europe's most dangerous person, following an elaborate scheme of deceit and the two-year period of questioning and imprisonment and a trial after the war had ended. He was clearly a foe but he also demonstrated the brave, bold and shrewd personality traits that the Mossad sought and needed who could be a bit closer than the Nazis.

Why did Skorzeny decide to collaborate with them? Skorzeny was able to escape from American security forces. It was reported that Skorzeny was assisted with The Office of Special Services, whom he later worked for. He traveled to Spain and eventually began to befriend Egyptian officers. The Mossad was planning to murder him, but Isser Harel chose to capture him through contact with him.

Mossad agent Raanan who was barely avoided the Holocaust was transferred to Germany to oversee operations, that focused upon German scientist in Egypt. His team sat and watched Skorzeny for a time before two men, who appeared German who walked up to him in a bar. They made a flimsy claim that they'd just been robbedand had losing everything, and Skorzeny invited them to his home.

Skorzeny was not fooled, however. He fired a gun at the couple and told them, "I know who you are and I understand the reason you're here. You're Mossad and you're here to take me down."

"You are only half-right. We're from Mossad however, should we have come to kill you we would have killed you just a few weeks ago."

"Or perhaps, I'd rather murder you."

"If you do us harm and we die, those who follow next won't be able to take a an alcoholic drink with you. You'll never even look at their faces as you blow your brains out. We're offering this offer only to assist with our efforts," said the agent with a substantial sum of money.

"I must get Wiesenthal to take my name off of his database," Skorzeny said. Skorzeny was identified as war criminal. The Mossad were willing to accept the terms of reference regardless of whether or not they believed they were able to keep their word. They required Skorzeny.

He was then taken by bus to Tel Aviv and introduced to Harel. Also, the group visited Yad Vashem Museum located in Jerusalem that is dedicated to commemorating the six millions Jewish survivors of the Holocaust This isn't part of the secret service's training however it is essential for Skorzeny's visit.

The Israelis weren't certain if they could trust Skorzeny However, he was able to provide intelligence about Egypt's military programs and kept in touch with Raanan.

Wiesenthal was unwilling to take Skorzeny off his war crimes list however, Mossad issued a statement stating the crime was committed regardless as well. Skorzeny continued to work with the Mossad, Krug's assassination was one of his assignments. They were obliged to go through whatever was necessary.

When two men were found guilty of making threats against the family of a scientist's in Switzerland the Premier David Ben-Gurion thought the negative public image was disastrous. Isser Harel quit in the wake of the incident. This highlights the importance of secrecy within the agencies. The Mossad did not want to admit the lengths that they went to in order to accomplish their objectives, to the point that director Peter resigned after it became apparent that he was not doing enough to protect the secrecy of the agency.

Skorzeny's involvement was controversial The whole process from the beginning and then the signing in the form of the document. It is possible to argue that the Mossad does not have any true Allies outside Israel. Based on this it is logical and not as controversial. They do not just assassinate the terror leaders as well as anyone who might help the enemy.

Chapter 6: Mordechai Vanunu

Mordechai Vanunu worked as one of the Israeli nuclear technician during the 1980's. Vanunu was also a peace advocate and became a member of with the "Movement to Advance Peace" in 1984. He was known for his opposition to the 1982 Lebanon conflict and also campaigned for equal rights for Arab Israelis.

Vanunu sparked suspicion within the nuclear plant's staff in 1984, when his travels across Europe and had a relationship with Arab students. In 1985, he lost his job, allegedly due to cuts to government budgets, but the labor union was able to win him back his job. It's not clear if these were actually the real reasons as well as if these were simply excuses made by the plant in order to discredit the man.

In his job, he secretly snapped photographsand quit the job on the 27th of October in 1985, in the wake of his bosses' efforts to assign him to jobs that were less sensitive than his prior posts.

Vanunu had a lot of travel. He visited Israel as well as his home country of the United States,

Greece, Thailand, Moscow, Burma, Mandalay, Nepal, before finally arriving in Sydney, Australia, where Vanunu came to. He was introduced to an Australian reporter from Colombia who convinced him to tell his story and photos. He first attempted to go to Newsweek before he was able to get The British Sunday Times. In September of 1986, he was interviewed by Sunday Times journalist Peter Hounam in London and it was unconstitutional to the non-disclosure contract he signed.

The paper verified the story by speaking to nuclear weapons experts. Vanunu shared details of the methods used to create various types of bombs. This led experts to suggest that Israel could produce around 150 nuclear bombs.

The Israeli government was alerted concerning Vanunu as a possible target and decided to seize Vanunu before the report was published, but they decided they had to force Vanunu to quit British territory by himself to remain in good relations with the Prime Secretary Margaret Thatcher.

Mossad thought it was an female agent to draw Vanunu away. Agent Cheryl Bentov posed as "Cindy," an American tourist and wooed him. He immediately became skeptical of her and inquired whether she was an official Mossad agent, however was still enticed. Many even claimed that Vanunu was "desperate to be a bride." Vanunu was aware of the Mossad however, she didn't be aware of what it could do till it got too much. Cindy was able to lure Vanunu to Rome to go on a trip.

"It was only after the Mossad people came after me in my apartment at Rome that I realized the truth the situation, although for a brief moment I thought I was also an innocent victim. After three days aboard the ship that took me to Israel I concluded that she was a part of the scheme."

He was correct. He was interrogated and questioned in authorities from the Mossad within Israel on October 6 just one day after The Sunday Times published the story. On March 28 1988, he was sentenced to treason and espionage and sentenced to 18 years in prison, during which he was sentenced to more than eleven years in isolated confinement. The government did do not wish to divulge any further Israeli nukes' secrets.

After his release from jail on April 21st 2004 he was subjected to various restrictions, the majority of which had to relate to international or online contact. The inmate was also not allowed for departure from his home in the State of Israel.

Many believe that Vanunu did not pose an actual security threat to Israel at the time he was detained. Vanunu's solitary confinement can be seen as another method of avoiding embarrassment in the political arena. It can also set a precedent and sends a message to those who possess secret information regarding Israel. There are those who believe that he was put in solitary confinement to strip him of his mental sanity. The Israeli government claims that Vanunu "not entirely there" as well as "imagines some things" However, Vanunu claims contrary. Vanunu says he doesn't regret sharing information with Sunday Times. Sunday Times.

Bull, Bseiso, and Shaqaqi

Canadian native Gerald Bull did a variety of research and development projects for Canadian as well as American program for missiles. He was a world-wide artillery expert with Space Research Corporation. Space Research Corporation. They sold the equivalent of 50,000 ERFB ammunition for Israel in 1973 to be used in American-made artillery pieces after which Bull was given American citizenship. They also made a few additional sales, however Bull was charged with illegal arms trading in 1977, since Bull had violated UN Security Council Resolution 418.

Bull relocated to Brussels and began his work with Brussels' European Poudreries Reunies of Belgium. Later , he began work with People's Republic of China, and Iraq. He created two artillery pieces for Iraqis and suggested building the cannon needed to launch rockets into space for the Iraqis. He also designed a 150-meter machine gun and offered to assist in the development of the Scud-based missile.

Bull's productivity with Iraq made him one of the many targets of the Mossad. In the months after, he agreed to work on the missile project. Following this agreement his apartment was broken into multiple times; a warning from Israel. In March or 1990 he was assassinated.

While many suspected the Mossad for the assassination, the agency supposedly had distributed false stories to European media, claiming Iraq agents shot Bull.

Still, Bull's cooperation with Saddam Hussein was a threat to both Israel and Iran (and other nations as well), and some also suspected that the CIA, M16, or the Chilean, Syrian, Iraqi, or South African government could have been behind the assassination.

Atef Bseiso was the PLO head of intelligence. He was assassinated in Paris in 1992. The PLO said that the Mossad was responsible, while the French police suspected the Palestinian Abu Nidal terrorist group.

Bseiso's death was considered a blow to the PLO's effort to build a relationship with France, so it was easy to see how it could be Mossad's doing. They had previously wanted to attack leaders to break down the PLO and other organizations that posed a threat to Israel. However, Israeli officials called this claim "dubious and imaginative," and that the killing could have resulted from "internal rivalries." They didn't deny their involvement in assassination of Fathi Shaqaqi, though.

Shaqaqi practiced medicine in Egypt and Jerusalem, then founded the Islamic Jihad Movement in Palestine in the early 1980's. He was also acquainted with Salah Sariya, a Palestinian who was executed in 1976 for plotting the assassination of the President of Egypt at the time, Ariwar Sadat. He believed that only an Islamist movement could achieve any political or military success against Israel. The Jihad Movement established a sovereign, Islamic Palestinian state that aimed to achieve its goals via military means.

In 1992, Shaqaqi said his aim was a Palestine from the river to the sea "where all religions can live together."

His secret organization, though, seemed to prove he thought differently. Shaqaqi's organization claimed to prohibit targeting innocent civilians, but these civilians did not include Israeli settlers. Their operations included assassinations, mass shootings, bombings, and suicide bombings of Israeli targets.

Shaqaqi was arrested by Israel multiple times, imprisoned in Israel, and deported to Southern Lebanon, before settling in Damascus in 1990. Five years later he was gunned down by Mossad agents, apparently the same two who killed Gerald Bull and Atef Bseiso.

Hamas Leaders

On July 30th, 1997, two Palestinian suicide bombers were carried out at the Mahane Yehuda Market in Jerusalem. 16 civilians (13 Israeli) were killed, and 178 were injured. Three died later from their injuries. On September 4th there was a triple suicide bombing on a pedestrian mall, also in Jerusalem. Five were killed and over 190 were injured.

The attacks were considered heroic by Fahad Rimawi, editor of the Jordanian weekly Almajd. They "gave meaning to Arab heroism. We do not hide our happiness upon this act." They were direct enemies of Israel.

In retaliation, the Mossad targeted Khalad Mashal, Palestinian political leader and the organization Hamas, which carried out the suicide bombings.

Two agents used fake Canadian passports to enter Jordan. They waited at the entrance of the Hamas offices and attempted to poison Mashal. However, the agents were captured, and Jordan's King Hussein demanded the antidote to the poison, saying that he would cut diplomatic relations and try the detained agents if it was not given.

Danny Yatom, head of Mossad at the time, brought the antidote to Mashal, however the doctors there had already administered a similar antidote.

"Israeli threats have one of two effects: some people are intimidated, but others become more defiant and determined. I am one of the latter," said Mashal afterwards.

Following the incident, spiritual leader of Hamas, Ahmed Yassin, was released from Isreal, along with more Palestinian and Jordanian prisoners.

This mission to eliminate Mashal was ultimately a failure. There were no casualties and the agents were released, but the operation cost Israel some of its prisoners, and of course money, resources, and time. Furthermore, Canadians were mad over the use of Canadian passports by the agents.

Later, Mashal also helped negotiate a prisoner exchange deal, which consisted of captured Israeli soldier Gilad Shalit in exchange for over 1,000 Palestinian prisoners in Israel. This was only one of his many influential actions as a leader. Mashal was the quintessential Mossad target. He was a clear enemy and the squad failed to kill him. In this situation the method of killing may have been questionable. The kinds of statements the Mossad tries to make in its methods of killing are ambiguous. If they could get close enough to poison him, why not just shoot him? Poison was probably a better choice for a public area. It would have been a cleaner kill, if they hadn't gotten caught immediately.

Izz El-Deen Sobhi Sheikh Khalil was also a senior member of the military wing of Hamas. He was deported by Israel to Lebanon in the early 1990s. He died on September 26th,

2004, when a booby-trap exploded in Damascus, Syria. This was the next killing blamed on the Israelis by both Hamas and Syria.

"We blame Mossad for putting a bomb in his car," Hamas spokesman Mushir al-Masri told the AFP new agency in Gaza city, while Israel's public security minister Gideon Ezra said he had no information.

"I can't confirm or deny it, [but] I'm not sorry this happened," he told Israeli television, giving the public a clear view of where he stood on the matter and providing the usual Mossad obscurity.

No one has taken responsibility for the assassination, as is the case in numerous other attacks and assassinations, however it is now considered another Mossad operation. There had been two bus bombings killing 16 civilians in Beersheba, Israel, only a month before, and the Israeli military said an assassination campaign against Hamas leaders would follow. Six years before, there was a grenade attack at the central bus station in the same city. Hamas claimed responsibility for several other suicide bombings, so many that there is even a whole Wikipedia page dedicated to Palestinian suicide bombings. This was certainly enough motive for the Mossad to retaliate.

Imad Mughniyah

Hezbollah, meaning "Party of Allah," is one of Israel's enemies based in Lebanon. Funded by Iran and consisting of mainly Shia Muslims, it harasses the Israeli occupation in south Lebanon.

Imad Mughniyah was a principal leader within the Hezbollah's military intelligence, and security apparatuses, after he was involved with Fatah. He was blamed for the Beirut barracks bombing and US embassy bombings in 1983, and for kidnapping dozens of foreigners in Lebanon in the '80s. He was also indicted in Argentina for participating in the 1992 Israeli embassy attack in Buenos Aires.

Dangerous and powerful, Mughniyah fit the profile for a Mossad target, but he was extremely difficult to track. He frequently changed identities, and even had plastic surgeries. He disguised himself in Western clothing and even masks. He was considered

Israel's most wanted terrorist, along with Hassan Nasrallah, another Hezbollah leader.

In 1990, Mossad tried to assassinate Mughniyah in Beirut, but ended up killing his brother instead. Mughniyah cautiously stayed away from the funeral. One could even argue that killing his brother was only a ploy to get him to the funeral, though it didn't work. The same year "he just disappeared completely," said Palestinian leader Mohammad Yassin, probably after knowing the deadly Mossad were out for him.

Israel was also assumed, by Syria and the Palestinians, to have been involved in terror attacks and assassination attempts on militants in Damascus, especially the Islamic Jihad. The long string of conflict between Israel and the Islamic Jihad was certainly justification for blaming the death of Mughniyah on the Mossad.

"Mugniyah is the one who has been pinpointed as the No. 1 hunted man ever since the 1983 Marine barracks bombing, as someone who was instrumental in conducting Hazbollah's foreign operations," Prof. Magnus

Ranstorp, of University of St. Andrews Center for the study of Terrorism, says.

He was also on the US State Department's list of most wanted terrorism suspects. They found him responsible for the deaths of more Americans around the world than anyone else. These included the 1983 suicide bombing that killed 241 US Marines in Lebanon, the 1983 bombing of the US embassy in Beirut, which killed 63, and the kidnapping of Western hostages in Beirut in the mid '80s. Hostages William Buckley, the CIA station chief in Beirut, and Lt. Col. William Higgins, who served with UN forces in Lebanon, were killed.

Mughniyah was "probably the most intelligent, most capable operative we've ever run across," said former CIA agent Robert Baer, who had been tracking him. The FBI was offering a $5 million reward just for information leading to Mughniyah's arrest.

Attempts by the US to eliminate Mughniyah dated all the way back to the 80's. In 1986 and 1995 they attempted and failed to take him from France and Saudi Arabia, respectively.

He finally died in an explosion in Damascus, Syria on February 12th, 2008. At the time, Israel broadcasted nationwide the death of "the most dangerous of terrorists in the Middle East in the past 30 years." It was assumed the Mossad were responsible, though the Israeli government said that the country "rejects the attempt by terror groups to attribute to it any involvement in this incident."

It could be assumed that the Mossad did careful planning to carry out the operation, but the killing was not quite as specific, for example, as the assassinations in the Wrath of God, where the squad made sure to let no innocent people die. It was not known how many people were killed and injured as Mughniyah died, but the stakes were higher than ever with this assassination. Many people did not even know what Mughniyah looked like, so we could guess this is one of the few chances they would have had to target him. We could also imagine the amount of intelligence required to find him.

The Mossad continues to deny involvement in the operation, despite the huge success the mission was for Israel and Western countries.

Later, a Mossad spy Ali Jarrah, who was charged with espionage for Israel, confirmed to investigators that he was assigned to scout the Kfar Soussa district in Damascus, where Mughniyah was. He also testified to having scouted "certain points" in northern Syria, where General Mohammad Suleiman was assassinated. This could be considered evidence that Israel was behind Mughiniyah's death, but there isn't enough proof.

"There is no doubt that General Mohammed Suleiman is the closest person to Bashar al-Assad and is his right hand in the armed forces and he knows everything," said an unidentified Syrian official. Suleiman was supposedly responsible for "sensitive security files" in the Syrian president's office and responsible for aspects of the army, and he may have been killed for knowing too much. He also transferred arms to the Hazbollah, making him a possible target for the Mossad.

Suleiman was reported killed by a sniper from a yacht on August 1st, 2008, the same year as Mughiniyah. Though many people and reporters assumed Israel was responsible, there was no definitive answer as to who was truly behind the attack. Some believed it had to do with internal fighting inside the Hezbollah, or that Bashar Assad may have wanted him killed for knowing too much information. Though Hezbollah blamed Israel for killing Mughiniyah, Damascus did not blame Israel for killing Suleiman. This put Israel in a good place, if it was in fact responsible, because it didn't feel like it needed to prepare for any revenge attacks.

Mahmoud Al-Mabhouh

Mahmoud Al-Mabhouh "never stopped thinking about how to fight the occupation by supplying quality weapons to the Palestinian fighters," explained Mohammed Nassar. He allegedly smuggled weapons from Iran to Gaza, an activity consistent with Mossad's other targets.

He joined the Muslim brotherhood in the late '70s in the Gaza Strip. Then his criminal activity began in the '80s, when he tried to sabotage coffee shops where people gambled. In 1986 he was arrested by Israeli security forces for having an assault rifle. After, he joined the military wing of Hamas. In 1989 he kidnapped and murdered two Israeli soldiers, and even celebrated it by standing on one of the corpses.

Undercover Israeli commandos tried to arrest him after, but he was able to flee to Gaza. Instead, his brother was arrested.

Al-Mabhouh smuggled hundreds of tons of arms of explosives from southern Iran to Egypt, and through Sinai and the tunnels under Rafah to the Gaza Strip.

To Israel, Al-Mabhouh was a threat, and he was a leader who they sought out to eliminate. We could also guess the Mossad wanted to take revenge for the killings of the Israeli soldiers. To get Al-Mabhouh would require extensive resources, though.

"The crime wouldn't have been that easy to commit, the culprits wouldn't have been able to hunt him down that easily," General Dahi Khalfan explained after the investigation of the death. His passport name was Abdul Raaouf Mohamed, and his travel plans were in no way available to anyone outside his inner circle. Khalfan thought Al-Mabhouh was betrayed by a Hamas member and the squad may have arrived in Dubai just 10 or 12 hours before him.

The police found more evidence than just motive that the Mossad was behind the attack, though. Lieutenant General Dahi Khalfan revealed that the Dubai Police had the DNA of four Mossad agents involved in the murder. How was this operation so much less discrete than the others?

Apparently there were around 26 agents on the team that carried out the operation. They needed this many people, or more, to be able to control the entire environment where the assassination was conducted, a style which adhered to the way military operations were conducted. They needed surveillance on the target, police, hotel staff, and a surrounding area so there was no chance for error. They took extreme care as to how the operation carried out, and arguably succeeded in carrying out the assassination by doing so.

Al-Mabhouh arrived in Dubai on January 19th, 2010 at 3 P.M. Some agents dressed as tennis players followed him into the elevator at some point, to get his room number. Then after learning this, another agent booked the room across the hall. At night, four men entered his room and killed him, though the exact, precise details were not determined.

The operation took less than 19 hours. Al-Mabhouh's brother, Faiq, said he was electrocuted and then strangled. Others say he was suffocated with a pillow. Hamas says he was tortured, and there were burn marks on his body.

Although they succeeded in eliminating Al-Mabhouh, the team did not conceal their faces in the operation, allowing cameras to catch them before and after they had on any disguises. Dubai authorities had their faces, though not their names, on closed-circuit TV cameras. Apparently one female agent even smiled at one of the cameras. From the recordings and other evidence, they were able to link the faces to the foreign passports, though these still gave away no information about the true agents' identities. Israel had underestimated the technology surrounding Al-Mabhouh, an embarrassment on their part.

It was presumed the Mossad were responsible.

Many organizations argue whether the assassination was really worth it. Furthermore, would they have still carried it out if Al-Mabhouh had not cruelly killed the two Israeli soldiers? The leader would be replaced, and others could certainly deal arms. The operation was considered by some a "serious policy failure." It was even more controversial because of the stolen identities.

Because it was presumed Mossad was responsible for the killing, many countries were outraged over its use of foreign passports. According to police in the country, the agency had not only used fake documents, but had used stolen identities of 32 Westerners to travel to Dubai. These included 12 British, eight Irish, and the rest from France, Australia and Germany. Many of the passports were said to be Israeli citizens with dual citizenship.

Britain expelled the Mossad station chief accredited to its embassy in London in March. Ireland decided to eject the Israel diplomat who came after official investigations. Australia warned Israel that this would compromise good relations between them. France and Germany were furious as well.

The operation caused many problems for the Mossad, but let's not forget what it accomplished for them. Ultimately, they succeeded in taking out a weapons dealer who was a threat to Israel.

Chapter 7: The Rise of the Mossad

As one of Israel's three major intelligence organizations, Mossad is responsible for intelligence gathering, intelligence analysis, covert operations in support of Israel's national defense and security, as well as protection of Jews around the world. Answering directly to the Prime Minister of Israel,[2] Mossad is responsible for meeting the state of Israel's Essential Elements of Information (EEI) requirements through human intelligence (intelligence gathered by interpersonal contact) and signals intelligence (intelligence gathered by interception of signals, such as radar or electronic communication between people or devices). Mossad formally acknowledges that its operatives use other methods to gather intelligence, noting that they are "not exposed publicly," for understandable reasons.[3]

Mossad is nominally modeled after the British Secret Intelligence Service (MI6) and the CIA, but it is unique in the degree to which it is believed to employ assassinations and covert operations in the place of war, as well as the degree of its operations with respect to non-

Israeli citizens of Jewish heritage.[4] Although MI6, the CIA, and the NSA are reportedly engaged in similar activities for their respective countries' national objectives, the degrees to which these organizations publicly acknowledge or promote such operations are significantly less than that of Mossad. Additionally, since Mossad and its predecessors had an outsized influence over policy decision-making from Israel's earliest days, the organization maintains closer ties to the government and has a stronger influence than its Western counterparts.[5]

During the British Mandate, the Haganah, a Jewish military force, developed an intelligence arm comprised of numerous, overlapping agencies and groups. One major line of effort within the nascent intelligence organizations was to thwart British intelligence's perceived efforts to plant spies inside the Jewish leadership and restrain the Jewish community from what the British government viewed as an aggressive expansion.[6]

As with most periods of Israeli history, there is a great deal of controversy about what happened during the British Mandate.

Mossad's official website states that during this time before the state's creation, Israeli intelligence services were developed primarily because "Arabs living in the Land of Israel…began violent actions against the Yishuv (the Jewish population)."[7] A CIA working paper declassified in 2007 states that in 1945 and 1946, the Strategic Services Unit (a CIA predecessor replacing the OSS) received reports from its European stations that a large-scale Jewish underground movement known as Brichah ("Escape") was taking place across European countries. This movement involved escorting Jews from Eastern Europe to safety in the West, with the end goal of resettling them in the Mandate of Palestine. The British saw this movement as a threat to their management of the territory and called for a restriction of Jewish migration to the area, driving the migration operation further underground.[8]

Controversial origins aside, conflicts between Israeli intelligence and military institutions and the British government instilled a propensity to favor asymmetrical and unconventional fighting techniques over conventional ones among the Israeli forces. The Palmach, a strike force of the Jewish Agency, as well as two Jewish "terrorist" organizations - the Irgun Zvai Leumi and Lochmei Heruth Israel - used these methods to successfully incur significant losses for the British military and security services between 1944 and 1948. The British Mandate set a status quo that would influence—and arguably hinder—the development of accountability mechanisms in Israeli intelligence, in part due to its state-of-emergency provisions to enforce order and suppress rebellions using extreme methods. Some believe that this state-of-emergency (the status of which has not been rescinded at the time of writing) has led to the establishment of extrajudicial institutions and a lack of true accountability for the government or its intelligence agencies.[9]

The Cold War ensured that Israel's alliances would be complicated from the start, and that events would involve the United States and Soviet Union. The United States Strategic Services Unit (SSU) became suspicious that Soviets were trying to infiltrate the Brichah in 1945, using it to smuggle Russian agents into the Middle East. In particular, a counter-intelligence report from Paris in February 1946 suggested that Soviets were using the Israeli intelligence organizations as a front for dispatching agents into British and American occupation zones in Germany and Austria. Kevin C. Ruffner explained that by "posing as Jewish victims of Nazi concentration camps, these agents were being processed through Allied displaced persons (DP) channels and the secret Jewish smuggling rings. The Soviet agents planned to spread rumors throughout Europe and in Palestine that the British hated the Jews and supported the Arabs for control of the Holy Land. Ultimately, according to an intelligence report given to the Americans by the French, the Soviets wanted to draw the Jews closer to Communism and incite them to revolt against the British in Palestine. In addition, the report listed the addresses of meeting places and the names of Jews in Austria involved in smuggling refugees."[10]

Other reports suggested that the Soviets provoked the Poles to attack Jewish civilians to discredit the Polish government and force the British to deal with the "Palestinian question."[11] The SSU thus sought to uncover Soviet efforts to influence Palestine and uncover Soviet smuggling routes, agents, and methods through what became known as "Project SYMPHONY." Major Edward P. Barry, chief of an SSU office in Paris, wrote that "this office began laying plans for a project which was to use the present extensive Jewish emigration for a source of CI information. Preliminary investigations on the subject plainly showed that no one in the American Forces in Austria had a clear picture of either the procedure or the agencies involved."

The project was headed by Jules Koenig, the son of Polish immigrants. Koenig saw SYMPHONY as a continuation of wartime collaborations between the Allies and the Jews, only this time in a fight against the Soviet Union, rather than Nazi Germany.[12] The project's short-term aim was to locate agents of the Jewish Agency's running emigration of Jews from Soviet satellite states and intelligence services and war criminals into those countries. Its intermediate aims were to locate people in official organizations, such as local Red Cross branches, who had provided false papers and identification cards for smugglers in those regions. Its long-term goals were to penetrate organizations sending Soviet-trained or "Russian-inspired" agents through the flow of Jewish refugees to further propaganda or gather intelligence in Allied (or ally-occupied) countries such as France, Italy, the U.S., and Palestine.[13]

Brichah leaders, many of whom would move to Israel and work for the Mossad or its predecessors, quickly learned that they could trust no one, even their allies. Indeed, Koenig and his team recruited a wide range of agents to spy on clandestine Israeli activities, including Arthur Pier, the leader of the Jewish Agency in Vienna and covert head of the Brichah in Austria, named Arthur Pier. Koenig and his team estimated that Pier had smuggled hundreds if not thousands of Jews on a monthly basis through Austria and eventually into Italy and Palestine. An SSU operative posed as a reporter and brokered a deal with Pier to pass intelligence on to the U.S.

Another agent recruited by the SSU was Wender, an Austro-Hungarian Jew who had been coerced into reporting for both German and British intelligence during the war. Arrested as a black marketeer by the

American military in Vienna in 1946, Wender was offered a position as a Project SYMPHONY agent. In exchange for his release from confinement, along with 750 shillings a month and rations, Wender agreed to be a conduit for clandestine collection on the Jewish Agency and penetration by the Soviets and the British.[14]

The United States' SSU had informants from inside the Jewish Agency such as Gideon Rafael, a German Jew who sought to establish formal ties between the Jewish Agency and American intelligence. In an effort to escalate the proposal, Rafael provided Koenig with inside information on the Jewish Agency's relations with the OSS during the war. Noting that the British and Americans had exploited the Jewish Agency during the war but had given it little credit for the information it had supplied the Allies, he offered the Americans the use of Jewish couriers in Eastern Europe in exchange for formalized cooperation. Historical accounts suggest that cooperation between agents like Rafael remained relatively informal, but they were, indeed, provided to the SSU and its successor, the CIA.[15]

Project SYMPHONY was ultimately shut down due to a lack of trust in the agents recruited, as well as the lack of American Yiddish-speaking investigators to analyze the activity of the covert Jewish population being moved about. It was deemed useless to participate in a large-scale human smuggling operation for the sake of intelligence-gathering with barriers such as this in place.[16] There are limited public Israeli accounts on the SSU's opportunistic support and attempted exploitation of Israel's emigration projects, but judging by the widespread attempted recruitment of Brichah agents, it is reasonable to suspect that by the end of Project SYMPHONY, there were several future Israeli leaders who had learned to deal with apparent U.S. allies with great circumspection.

Restrictions imposed on Jewish immigration to Palestine remained in place throughout World War II and continued in the aftermath, even as millions of displaced Jews throughout Europe sought sanctuary from the horror of the Holocaust, the true extent of which was only then being fully appreciated. There was an obvious unwillingness on the part of many

East European Jews to return to their ruined communities, and a mass movement of Jews within and out of Europe began. The British established a quota of 18,000 a year, which all but made legal immigration impossible for the hundreds of thousands of Jews trying to get into Palestine. Thousands were intercepted and interred in camps in Cyprus.

A Jewish underground movement began to facilitate illegal immigration from Europe and elsewhere to Palestine, under the codename Aliyah Bet. The program, in fact, began before the war, as the British began attempting to limit Jewish arrivals in order to try and defuse tensions, but it was curtailed during the war since maritime transit was impossible under wartime conditions. The effort to accelerate Jewish immigration was naturally motivated by the horrors of the Holocaust and European anti-Semitism in general, but it was also part of a strategy to improve the demographic balance as much as possible in favor of the Zionists at a time when Zionist militias were beginning to exchange blows with the British Army. The British did what they could to enforce the restrictions imposed in the 1939 White Paper, but a great many immigrant ships sidestepped the blockade, and tens of thousands of Jews were able to enter Palestine illegally and settle.

Hostilities between Arabs and Jews, and between Zionist Militias and the British Army, began again in earnest after the war, and they escalated quickly. The British soon found themselves under pressure from all sides, and the United States, under President Harry S. Truman, urged the lifting of Jewish immigration restrictions and limits on Jewish land purchases. This led to the establishment of an Anglo-American Committee of Inquiry, which, in April 1946, opened the way for the legal entry of 100,000 Jewish Holocaust survivors and the rescinding of restrictions of land sales to Jews. It further suggested that the territory of Palestine be neither Jewish nor Arab, urging instead a continuation of international trusteeship.

These recommendations, forlorn in their optimism, triggered violent demonstrations in the neighboring Arab states, and some called for a Jihad and an annihilation of all European Jews in Palestine. At the end of 1946, upwards of 600,000 Jews were known to reside in the Mandate of Palestine, compared to a population of 1,300,000 Arabs.

Britain, now facing the reality of decolonization and the winding down of the British Empire, rapidly lost its appetite to deal with what was an increasing intractable problem, so in February 1947, the British announced their intention to relinquish the governing mandate over the territory of Palestine. By then, the League of Nations had been superseded by the United Nations as the global governing body, and the matter was therefore submitted to the General Assembly to be resolved. The British anticipated a single-state solution and was quietly hopeful that the Arab majority population would carry the day. The United States, on the other hand, now more forceful in international affairs, pressed for a solution more favorable to the Jews.

In May 1947, a United Nations Special Committee, UNSCOP, was established to investigate and make recommendations for the future of Palestine. The Jewish Agency lobbied for Jewish representation on the committee, and also, in a sign of a more hawkish and confident Zionist mood, for the exclusion of both Britain and Arab countries. It also pressed hard for the committee to include visits to camps where Holocaust survivors were interned in Europe as part of its brief. The Arab states, on the other hand, convinced that Arab statehood in Palestine was under threat, and unwilling to acknowledge the United Nations justification over the matter, argued that the rule of Palestine should revert to its inhabitants, in accordance with the provisions of the Charter of the United Nations, or that the matter should be put before an International Court. The Arab Higher Committee, therefore, refused to cooperate with UNSCOP.

In August 1947, a majority report of the United Nations Special Committee recommended that the region be partitioned into separate Arab and Jewish states. This was followed, on November 29, 1947, by a vote of the United Nations General Assembly that ratified the plan, and put it into existence. The terms of the plan were contained in Resolution 181, and the most important result was that the land would be partitioned in such a way as to ensure that each state would have a majority of its own population.

Nonetheless, inevitably, some Jewish settlements would fall within the proposed Arab state, while hundreds of thousands of Palestinian Arabs would become part of the proposed Jewish state. The area designated for the Jewish state would also be slightly larger than the Arab state, in the expectation of accelerated Jewish immigration at the moment that Jewish autonomy was achieved. Jerusalem and Bethlehem would become international zones under United Nations administration.

While that partition sounds lopsided at first glance, it's important to recall, as Zionists at the time pointed out, that Transjordan, which was granted independence by the British in 1946, had comprised 75% of the entire land under British control, meaning the proposed Jewish state would end up comprising less than 15% of the entire Mandate while two Arab countries got the other 85%. Publicly, the Zionist Jewish leadership accepted this plan, acknowledging it as "the indispensable minimum." The Arabs, on the other hand, rejected the plan entirely, regarding the whole process, including the General Assembly vote, as an international betrayal.

Ongoing tensions and clashes flared into organized communal violence at the moment that the General Assembly vote was made public and the partition plan was formally adopted. Bombings, killings and riots became a matter of daily life on both sides, although on the whole, the Jews tended to more frequently be on the receiving end. According to Israel Galili, Chief of Staff of the Haganah, "As far as we know, it is the Mufti's belief that there is no better way to 'start things off' than by means of terror, isolated bombs thrown into crowds leaving movie theaters on Saturday nights. That will start the ball rolling. For no doubt the Jews will react, and as a reaction to a reaction there will be an outbreak in another place ... until the whole country will be stirred up, trouble will be incited, and the neighboring Arab countries will be compelled to start a 'holy war' to assist the Palestinian Arabs."

Clearly, the Higher Arab Council hoped, through an organized campaign of violence, that a wider regional conflict would be sparked. Attacks, however, were often random and uncoordinated, utilizing poorly armed, ill-trained and disorganized militias, contrasting sharply to the Haganah, which, although numerically inferior, was motivated, organized, trained, and reasonably well-armed. In fact, the importation of armaments, especially heavy arms, was difficult, if not impossible, so long as the British were in substantive control of Palestine. In December 1947, Zionist leader David Ben-Gurion ordered the Haganah to begin transitioning into a regular army in expectation of an escalation of the violence, but the emphasis tended to be on the training and organization of manpower, and the establishment of communications networks and command and control. Meanwhile, arms were purchased overseas and held in readiness to be introduced as soon as the British had relinquished control. Soon afterwards, Zionist forces abandoned their defensive posture and began staging retaliatory raids and offensive actions against hostile Palestinian villages and mounting regular assassinations of Palestinian militia and civic leaders.

David Ben-Gurion giving the declaration of Israel's independence

On May 14, 1948, Ben-Gurion, as the head of the Jewish Agency, declared the establishment of the State of Israel, and the following day the British Mandate of Palestine officially expired. As the British packed up and left the territory, no doubt breathing a sigh of relief, the armies of four Arab nations – Egypt, Syria, Transjordan and Iraq – entered what had been British Mandatory Palestine, triggering the 1948 Arab-Israeli War. Ostensibly, the Arab forces embarked on the war to reverse the creation of Israel in defense of the Palestinians, but it is also likely that each held its own territorial ambitions, and it is probably unlikely that an Arab victory would have resulted in the formation of a Palestinian state.

Given the numbers on each side, it seemed the new Israeli state was facing staggering odds, so it's no surprise that what followed was quite sobering to Israel's Arab neighbors. In less than a year, they would be repelled and defeated with comparative ease, which, bearing in mind the disparity of weapons and manpower that the two sides wielded, shocked them to the core.

During May and June of 1948, when the fighting was at its most intense, the balance was very much in doubt, but as arms shipments began to reach Israeli fighting formations, the Israeli Defense Force gradually began to dominate the battlefield. Much of the reason for this was a lack of tactical coordination between the individual Arab armies, each of which fought an individual campaign in individual sectors.

The Israelis began pressing their advantages on both land and air by the fall of 1948, bombing foreign capitals like Damascus while overrunning Arab armies locally. In towns like Ramat Rachel and Deir Yassin, close quarter combat in villages led to civilian casualties and charges of massacres. In particular, the Jewish assault on Deir Yassin, which led to the death of about 50 Palestinians, is often labeled a massacre by the Palestinians, while the Israelis asserted that house-to-house combat made fighting difficult. Regardless, Palestinians who heard of the news of Jewish attacks on places like Deir Yassin were afraid for their lives and began to flee their homes. At the same time, Palestinians were encouraged by commanders of the Arab armies to clear out of the area until after they could defeat Israel. Palestinians and Jews had been fighting since 1947, and over 250,000

Palestinians had already fled their homes by the time the war had started. It is unclear how many Palestinians fled from Jewish forces and how many left voluntarily, but by the end of the war, over 700,000 Palestinians had fled from their homes. Meanwhile, nearly 800,000 Jews had been forcibly expelled from their homes in nations throughout the Middle East, leading to an influx of Jews at the same time Palestinians were leaving.

By late 1948, Israel was on the offensive. That December, the U.N. General Assembly passed Resolution 194, which declared that under a peace agreement, "refugees wishing to return to their homes and live in peace with their neighbors should be permitted to do so," and "compensation should be paid for the property of those choosing not to return."

Protracted peace talks began late in January 1949, resulting in individual armistices signed with each defeated power. Iraq did not sign an armistice, instead merely opting to withdraw its forces. The territory once known as Palestine was divided into three parts, each under a different political regime. Israel now encompassed over 77% of the lands that were part of the U.N. Partition Plan, while Jordan held East Jerusalem and the West Bank, and Egypt occupied the coastal strip adjacent to the city of Gaza.

The Palestinian Arab state, central to the partition plan, was never realized, not least because of the number of Palestinians who left the region before and during the war. The War of Independence, as it is known by the Israelis, and the Nakba, or the Catastrophe, as it is known by the Arabs, incorporates the entire period of hostilities between late 1947 and early 1949, including a period of low-level hostilities and attrition during which many Palestinian Arabs were forced from their homes or chose to flee. Prior to the involvement of neighboring Arab states, and the open war that followed, the nature of the developing conflict involved reciprocating attacks and reprisals between isolated Arab and Jewish settlements, intertwined with one another on a landscape under rapid social evolution. Typically, ad hoc Arab militias would launch attacks, which would be followed by reprisals staged by ad hoc Jewish militias aiming to deter future aggression.

As Israel fought for its independence, Israeli intelligence fought for its ability to function as a trustworthy, reliable entity. The first notable head of Israeli intelligence was Isser Be'eri, a Poland-born construction company director who was appointed the head of the Shai, the early intelligence branch of the Haganah prior to Israel's declaration of independence on May 14, 1948. Israel's leaders found themselves threatened on all sides by their neighbors during the Israeli War for Independence, and for a young country in desperate need of heroes, Be'eri was initially praised as a strong leader with a formidable drive to protect the citizens of the new nation.

Be'eri

However, Be'eri's methods of quashing internal threats were immediately recognized as draconian and morally questionable. Be'eri astonished Prime Minister Ben-Gurion when he showed him confidential telegraphs his men had intercepted that revealed Abba Hushi, an influential leader and political ally of Ben-Gurion, had collaborated with British intelligence. He additionally ordered the arrest and torture of Hushi's friend, Jules Amster, who was released after refusing to betray Hushi. Amster was toothless and covered in scars after 76 days.[17]

In June 1948, Be'eri ordered the hasty trial and death by firing squad of Captain Meir Tobianski, who had been suspected of colluding with a British national to empower the Jordanian Army's shelling of strategic targets throughout Jerusalem. An inquiry into the incident revealed that Be'eri had been guilty of ordering the forgery of the telegraphs that incriminated Hushi, as well as bypassing the judiciary system for Tobianski's condemnation and execution. He was also found guilty of the unauthorized assassination of Ali Kassem, whom he suspected was an enemy of the state.

Prime Minister Ben-Gurion acted immediately by ordering Be'eri tried in a military court, leading him to be stripped of rank and dishonorably discharged from the IDF.[18] He was then tried by a civil court, which found him guilty of manslaughter and sentenced him to one day in prison, "from sunrise to sunset, 30 days after sentencing." This punishment is seen to have been largely symbolic, and President Chaim Weizmann pardoned him before it was carried out.[19]

During his trial, Be'eri told the court-martial, "The moment an intelligence service begins to act according to law, it will cease to be an intelligence service."[20]

Some analysts believe that following the incident, the secret service placed nominal limits on its power and based future operations on legal and moral principles designed with the intent of preserving individual rights. Others have argued that through the Mossad's clandestine nature, Ben-Gurion prevented the creation of a legal basis for Mossad's operations. Thus, while internal laws might have existed to lay out its goals, missions, powers, and budgets, there was little transparency or observable external accountability, at least in the early days.[21]

In April 1948, the Supreme Inter-Service Coordination Committee was established, and Reuven Shiloah, the son of a rabbi and Ben-Gurion's confidant and advisor, was appointed to lead it. The committee later became the Heads of Services Committee and included the Shin Bet, formulated from the Shai, the State Department, the military intelligence department, and the Israeli Police. Shiloah's challenge was to unite these disparate groups, increasing their effectiveness and accountability in the process.

Shiloah

Shiloah was doubtless helped by his experience in clandestine activity and deal-brokering. He had spent three years in Baghdad, posing as a journalist and learning about Iraq's political, economic, and military power structures and inner-workings. Additionally, he helped to execute an influence campaign over the Iraqi press, and he later noted, "The Arabic Press is almost entirely under the influence of the Jewish Community," and urge the Jewish Agency's Political Department to "explain to their Committee what I want them to get into the Arab papers."[22] Part of this influence campaign was to convince Iraqi Jews to immigrate to Palestine, both legally and illegally, and train them.

During World War II, he negotiated with the British to set up a Jewish Commando Corps to sabotage operations in Nazi Europe. One of the units posed as German battalion and another as an Arab battalion. On top that, he arranged for the British to parachute Jewish volunteers from Palestine into occupied Europe to organize local Jewish resistance and establish contacts with the precursor to the CIA.[23]

In Israel Shiloah had his work cut out for him. A CIA report noted that competition among the intelligence services led to conflict between the intelligence apparatus's early founders. In particular, Shiloah clashed with Arthur Pier, the former member of the Jewish Agency in Vienna and head of the Birchah of Austria who had since moved to Israel and changed his name to "Asher Ben-Natan," as well as Boris Guriel, who had served as head of the political department of the Shai. These men frequently argued with Shiloah about organizational, strategic decisions.[24] Shiloah found this infighting exhausting, and he haggled with Ben-Gurion for months to place all intelligence under his control.[25] Shiloah made this campaign of consolidation formal in July 1949 and proposed taking the establishment of a Central Institute for Coordination of the Intelligence and Security Services. Ben-Gurion approved this proposal and appointed Shiloah the head of the new

"Institute" (in Hebrew, "Mossad") on December 13, 1949.[26]

Ben-Natan

Shiloah used the reputation and leadership skills gained from his operational experience to overcome considerable bureaucratic resistance, including firing intelligence service members who resisted the merger and replacing them with loyal agents who helped make the organization operational in a little over a year. In March 1951, after Shiloah effectively fired Boris Guriel from the State Department's Political Department, Guriel waged a "spies revolt" in which Ben-Natan and other members of the Political department resigned in protest and destroyed their records instead of turning them over to the new Mossad.[27]

In spite of this infighting and internal sabotage, Shiloah is viewed as being at least partly successful in making Mossad a central body coordinated between three existing security groups: the military intelligence (AMAN); the Internal Security Service (Shin Bet); and the state department's political intelligence department. From the beginning,

Mossad was designed to be hidden from the Israeli public, and mentioning the Shin Bet or Mossad in public was prohibited until the 1960s.[28]

Cold War Dynamics

In addition to gaining internal control over the previously disparate branches of Israeli intelligence and establishing legitimacy within his team, Shiloah enabled the first formal U.S.-Israel agreement on intelligence and cooperation in May 1951.[29] This was no small feat, as the Americans remained concerned the Soviets had "penetrated the infrastructure of the Israeli intelligence and security services."[30] Israel was indeed being armed by the Communist bloc at that time, but Shiloah saw eventual membership in NATO as essential to Israel's long-term interests, and he enabled it through behind-the-scenes deals made by members of the intelligence community.[31]

However, regardless of whether the organization itself remained a secret, Mossad's early operations were quickly found out. In 1951, one of Mossad's spy rings in Baghdad was exposed, triggering the arrest of officers and the persecution of Jews in Baghdad.[32] Ultimately, thousands of Jews had to be airlifted from Baghdad to Israel, but many who were left behind were tortured or killed as tensions between Iraq and Israel escalated.

There were other failed operations under Shiloah's auspices which continued to discredit Mossad. For example, in December 1951, Dan Pines of the Labour newspaper Davar convinced Shiloah to fund an "intelligence network" in the Soviet Union, but he ultimately embezzled the money.[33]

Shiloah resigned in September of 1952, and his friends and rivals viewed the resignation as proof of Shiloah's being a poor fit for the position. Many saw him as an "ideas man," rather than an "organization man." The events in Baghdad, combined with a traffic accident and serious head injuries, had worn him down. In a diary entry, Prime Minister Ben-Gurion wrote, "I believe that Reuven has failed at his task…he fought the battle and dreamt the dream of Israel's resurgence only to burn himself out on the altar of his dream."[34] According to historian Haggai Eshed, however, the main reason for Shiloah's resignation was an ongoing campaign against him waged by rival Isser Harel, whom Ben-Gurion would appoint as Shiloah's successor in 1952. Eshed claimed that Harel kept close tabs on Shiloah, waging an influence campaign on Ben-Gurion to convince him that Shiloah was failing at his post.[35] This is one of many instances of infighting and internal sabotage in Mossad's early days.

Harel

Nicknamed "Little Isser," Harel was born in the ancient fortress town of Dvinsk in Russia, and after immigrating to Israel around the age of 18, Harel joined the Haganah during World War II and became the head of the Shai's Jewish Department, which tracked traitors and dissidents. After that, he became head of the Internal Security Service, known as the Shabak.

Under "Little Isser," Mossad expanded into five services: Mossad; Shabak; Aman (military intelligence); a special division of the police; and a research division of the foreign ministry. Michael Bar-Zohar nicknamed Isser "Israel's intelligence tsar" because he maintained effective control over the Shabak in addition to Mossad and played an outsized role in shaping Israeli intelligence during his tenure.[36]

Harel also helped to strengthen Mossad-CIA relations and is remembered as the man who gave the CIA the text of Nikita Khrushchev's 1956 speech denouncing Joseph Stalin. The text had been distributed to sister Communist parties in Eastern Europe, then passed on to the Israelis by Viktor Grayevsky, a Jewish journalist for a Polish Communist newspaper. The Americans, who had been "desperately" seeking a copy of the speech, were extremely grateful for this favor, and some have called the episode "the beginning of a beautiful friendship" between the Israeli and United States intelligence communities.[37]

That said, Harel's leadership was not the silver bullet for all of Mossad's challenges. Although the institution gained increasing prestige, they continued to experience internal sabotage. For example, it became clear that Israel Beer was, in fact, a Soviet mole. Beer had presented himself as an Austrian Jew when he joined the Haganah in 1938, and he acquired military and intelligence experience through the organization up until 1949. He remained in the role of chair of military history and was one of Ben Gurion's most trusted defense advisors until his arrest in 1961. Harel led an investigation discovering that Beer had actually been born with a different name and took the identity of the real Israel Beer when Beer died in the war. Based on these findings, Beer was convicted and sentenced to 15 years in prison, where he died.[38]

Eichmann

"He would leap laughing into the grave because the feeling that he had five million people on his conscience would be for him a source of extraordinary satisfaction." A subordinate on trial at Nuremberg paraphrased a boast of SS-Obersturmbannfuhrer Otto Adolf Eichmann with these words, summarizing the mood and character of Adolf Hitler's most notorious lieutenant for all posterity. A serial killer in earth-gray uniform and polished jackboots, Eichmann found an unprecedented opportunity for unleashing his homicidal impulses during the Final Solution from 1942-1945 at the height of the Nazi Third Reich's rule in Germany.

Historians once portrayed Eichmann mostly as a colorless, unimaginative bureaucrat who carried out the Holocaust simply because he lacked the imagination to reject the crime. Essentially "banal," this version of Eichmann turned him into a compliant functionary who handled the ghastly matter of collecting, transporting, and murdering millions of people with the same bland methodical means that other administrators applied to supplying the Wehrmacht with bread rations or new boots.

However, a closer examination of historical documents by other historians such as Bettina Stangneth led to a recent reevaluation of Eichmann. This perhaps more plausible reconstruction of the man reveals a driven hunter rejoicing in his power over his terrified quarry, an individual at once cruel, melodramatic, energetic, and cunning. Eichmann also used his fearsome reputation to carve out a political niche far more influential than his nominal rank – the equivalent of a lieutenant colonel – ordinarily offered. Even when he was captured and in the midst of his enemies, Eichmann showed a keen enjoyment of mental cat-and-mouse games, attempting to outmaneuver his accusers in a manner highly reminiscent of the slippery transformations utilized by manipulative killers such as Ted Bundy.

Eichmann during World War II

After the war, Eichmann concealed himself for several years in Lunenburg Heath in Bavaria, working in forestry under the name of Otto Heninger and trying to remain out of sight. In 1950, with the aid of an Austrian bishop who was sympathetic to the Nazis, he escaped to Argentina, setting the stage for one of the 20th century's most dramatic manhunts.

A fair number of Nazi officials, officers, and war criminals fled to Argentina before Eichmann journeyed there, creating a sort of expatriate enclave of Third Reich murderers tacitly shielded by the Argentine government. Juan Domingo Peron, the president of Argentina, showed mild sympathy for the Nazi government and arranged for his nation to provide a safe haven for fleeing Germans. Paradoxically, he also welcomed Jews to Argentina at the same time, so the Jewish and Nazi populations for the South American country both rose sharply during the late 1940s and into the early 1950s.

Josef Mengele, the "Angel of Death" who carried out grotesque, torturous, and usually fatal human medical experiments at Auschwitz-Birkenau, was one of the most infamous Nazis to reach South American shores, and his success likely encouraged other Nazis to put their trust in the secret "pipeline" arranged by sympathetic Catholic prelates to assist their exit from Europe. The black-mustached doctor and torturer managed to elude all capture attempts and ultimately drowned at the age of 67 while swimming at a pleasant seaside resort in 1979.

Mengele

Meanwhile, the hunt for Adolf Eichmann had begun in earnest even before World War II officially ended. Simon Wiesenthal, the famous Austrian Nazi hunter who later claimed far more credit for Eichmann's capture than he was actually due, began seeking the SS-Obersturmbannfuhrer almost immediately, and the Americans interviewed the captured, alias-shielded Eichmann twice because they were suspicious of who he truly was. Eichmann was already a highly wanted criminal.

Another factor that may have compelled Eichmann to leave for South America was the existence of small, unofficial Jewish squads who carried out vigilante murders against men whom they mistakenly believed to be Eichmann. "Five Jewish avengers, outfitted with British army uniforms and Sten guns [...] rammed their shoulders into the chalet door, bursting it open. They leveled their guns at the four defenseless men [...] Two men dragged [a German] out of the house [...] They carried him back to their Jeep and drove several miles into the pine forest. [...] [The] avengers fired several rounds of bullets into his chest. They cursed his very existence, then buried him in an unmarked grave. Adolf Eichmann was still very much alive the morning after the five Jewish avengers shot the man in Austria." (Bascomb, 2009, 53-55).

Eichmann eventually read a newspaper account of the vigilante murder carried out against the man mistakenly believed to be him. He appeared to be greatly amused by the story, and he even evinced pleasure at the report's description of how the luckless German shot in his stead defied his killers bravely. Eichmann seemed to think this redounded to his credit, as though the courage of his stand-in somehow represented his own valor as well.

Who provided exact information on Adolf Eichmann's precise whereabouts in the late 1950s remains a mystery to this day, but two main theories exist that attempt to explain how Israeli intelligence first ascertained Eichmann's location and alias.

One story, originating with Isser Harel, the leader of the Mossad at the time of Eichmann's abduction, asserts that Sylvia Hermann, the daughter of Dachau survivor Lothar Hermann, began a romantic relationship with one of Eichmann's sons. This led to Lothar Hermann reporting Eichmann's location in exchange for a substantial cash reward. The other story asserts that information provided by Simon Wiesenthal gave Israeli intelligence the clues required to track down Eichmann through careful detective work and a dash of luck.

The Sylvia Hermann story is quite popular among historians, perhaps because the detail of a romantic connection between Nick Eichmann and the Jewish daughter of a Holocaust survivor possesses such grim operatic irony. According to Harel's account, an Israeli agent, Efraim Hofstaetter, traveled to Argentina after a tip to speak with Lothar Hermann. Harel placed these words in the mouth of Sylvia Hermann's father: "I have a daughter – a charming girl, you'll meet her, she'll be home soon – a sensible and intelligent girl. [...] Until eighteen months ago, we lived in Buenos Aires, in the Olivos quarter. There she met a young man of twenty-one or twenty-two, named Nicolas Eichmann. He started taking her out and visited our house several times. Naturally, he didn't know that I have Jewish blood [...] So Nicolas used to talk freely in our company." (Harel, 1975, 18).

Though an incautious relationship has been the downfall of many criminals, spies, and other people in dangerous situations, two important sources tend to refute Harel's account. Lothar Hermann himself was alive when Harel's book was published, to the immense embarrassment of the Mossad leader. He responded to its claims with unrestrained fury, insisting that he did not think any Jew could lie as much as Harel. The other is Nicolas Eichmann himself, who, though willing to speak about his father and generally taking his side, never showed any signs of feeling personal guilt for Eichmann's unmasking.

If Harel's statement should not be taken at face value, neither should Lothar Hermann's vehement denials and outrage. It is a verifiable fact that Efraim Hofstaetter traveled to Argentina in early 1958 and arranged for a payment of 15,000 pesos to Lothar Hermann. Lothar sent Sylvia away to the United States shortly thereafter to attend a university there, but that may also have been an effort to remove her from Argentina in case violence erupted over the Eichmann affair.

Either way, what does seem certain is that Lothar Hermann contacted the West German state prosecutor Fritz Bauer with information about Eichmann. Bauer then telephoned Harel in Israel, and Harel sent Hofstaetter to investigate. From there, Hofstaetter interviewed Lothar Hermann and possibly his daughter (who did not leave for the United States until 1959).

Initially, however, Hermann made an error and gave Hofstaetter the name of the man who Eichmann rented his city residence from, Francisco Schmitt, instead of Eichmann's actual alias of Ricardo Klement. At this point, Israeli intelligence gave up on the lead, and though there is no precise information as to why, it seems likely that Hofstaetter investigated Francisco Schmitt and realized almost immediately that this individual was not Eichmann. Fritz Bauer, the West German prosecutor, did not give up so easily, but from the Mossad's perspective in early 1958, the meeting with Lothar Hermann failed to produce any information of value. Harel apparently glossed over this fact later to remove Simon Wiesenthal from the record and redirect all credit for the capture to himself.

The Nazi hunters tightened the net around Eichmann somewhat in the late 1950s, but his capture was by no means a foregone conclusion. In fact, it was an extraordinary achievement that occurred only through hard work, a large amount of luck, the courage of a few individuals, and an abduction plan straight from the pages of a Cold War era spy thriller. As opposed to the kind of tabloid journalism carried on by Isser Harel, Sylvia Hermann was only a tiny link in much more complex and fascinating web of circumstances.

The man who set the stage for Eichmann's capture was not an Israeli but a West German. Fritz Bauer, the judge who transmitted Lothar Hermann's tip to Isser Harel and the Mossad, did not give up as easily as the Israelis. Wiesenthal sent the judge information about Eichmann's probable hiding place in South America in the early 1950s, and Hermann's tips in late 1957 rekindled Bauer's interest in the case. Furthermore, Bauer spent the late 1950s campaigning for West Germany to issue arrest warrants and carry out trials of the long-neglected Nazi war criminals still lurking in South America, the Middle East, and even Europe itself.

Bauer

The catalyst prompting West Germany to accede to Bauer's wishes emerged from Cold

War politics. East Germany began a vigorous propaganda campaign against the West, questioning why the West Germans failed to prosecute Nazi war criminals more actively. The East Germans hinted darkly that their Western counterparts were, in fact, still National Socialists under the skin and would turn on NATO at some point in the future.

West Germany's allies did not respond very strongly to these communist jabs, likely dismissing them mostly as what they were, a transparent effort to drive a wedge between the Warsaw Pact's adversaries. The West Germans, however, were sufficiently alarmed enough to find their consciences again after overlooking the Nazi war criminals for over a decade. Having tasted the fruits of prosperous democracy and peace, they had no wish to risk their alliance for the sake of a few aging murderers. Accordingly, the West German government began issuing warrants, conducting arrests, and seeking to cooperate with other interested parties in ferreting out the most notorious SS men and others still at large.

The final clue spurring West Germany and Israel into action came from Simon

Wiesenthal, who was still monitoring Eichmann's relatives. When Maria Eichmann, Adolf's stepmother, died, her obituary in April 1959 listed "Vera Eichmann" as one of the survivors. Wiesenthal deduced from this that Adolf Eichmann was still alive because the last name suggested Vera had not remarried. He passed his suspicions and copies of the obituary to the Israeli consulate in Austria and a number of his fellow Nazi hunters, including several of his bitter rivals.

The report took several months to percolate upward through Israeli government channels, but eventually, it landed on the desk of the Mossad chief. Harel had previously ignored Wiesenthal's other research, dismissed Lothar Hermann's tip-off as worthless, and disregarded repeated messages from the West German government regarding Eichmann's location, but this time, Harel decided to act on the information. "He went to Prime Minister Ben-Gurion and told him: 'We have proof that Eichmann is in Argentina. Can I give orders for my men to get on his track?' – 'Yes,' said Ben-Gurion, 'bring back Eichmann dead or alive. But I'd rather you brought him back alive. It would have great meaning for young people.'" (Levy, 2002, 147).

Harel attempted to keep matters quiet while he set up his operation against Eichmann, but once again, enthusiastic amateur Nazi hunters proved to be a fly in the ointment. Precisely at the moment when Harel sought to keep mention of Eichmann at a minimum so as not to alarm his quarry, a fresh rumor set the Israeli news services blaring. Harel explained, "On October 11th, 1959, a sensational piece of news was published in the Israeli press: Eichmann was in Kuwait, working for an oil company. [...] The newspapers got their teeth into the subject and didn't let go for weeks. There were reports about teams of investigators in various countries working to find Eichmann. [...] I decided the best thing to do under the circumstances was to encourage the rumors about his being in Kuwait." (Harel, 1975, 31).

Harel's reasoning was that if he built up the Kuwait story, Eichmann and his associates would dismiss it as another groundless fable and remain in place, and given that Eichmann did not flee, Harel's plan likely worked.

Once they put the plan in motion, the Mossad sent three agents to Argentina with cameras in order to determine if the family living at 4261 Chacabuco Street was indeed that of the infamous Eichmann. These men rented a house exactly opposite Eichmann's dwelling and set about photographing him at every opportunity. The Israelis knew that Argentina would never extradite Eichmann, and if they broached the matter through official channels, their target would learn of their interest and vanish.

Of course, to make abduction the last bit justifiable, the Israelis needed conclusive evidence that their target was truly who they believed he was. If they abducted an innocent man based on rumor, Israel's standing in the international community would become that of a pariah. It was for this reason that the Mossad took extraordinary precautions to ascertain whether Ricardo Klement was indeed Adolf Eichmann in disguise.

Despite the precautions, the three Israeli Mossad agents were notably, even risibly, incompetent, according to Peter Z. Malkin, one of their colleagues. "Aside from very basic procedural errors […] they had made some gaffes that seemed almost beyond invention. One evening they actually overturned a Jeep on a quiet street only blocks away from the Klement house. Worse [...] they concocted a cover story [...] that they were canvassing the area as representatives of a North American firm [and] actually approached Klement's own daughter-in-law with this ludicrous tale." (Malkin, 1990, 119). Indeed, that story failed to match up with the situation since Chacabuco Street was a very poor spot for a factory due to its lack of water resources and scanty electricity. Many other spots in Buenos Aires would have made a far better place for a factory, a fact obvious to any local.

Even bigger mistakes followed when the Mossad agents betrayed the fact that they were not Americans at all. "When she overheard them speaking English, she switched to that language herself. And since she spoke it better than they did, they were obliged to beat a disorderly retreat." (Malkin, 1990, 119).

Nevertheless, Eichmann remained at Chacabuco Street for several more months until he moved to a house on Garibaldi Street that he and his sons constructed out of brick. A follow-up visit to the Chacabuco Street address by agent Zvi Aharoni, carrying a cigarette lighter as an anonymous gift to "Klaus Eichmann," or Nicolas Eichmann, the SS man's son, revealed that the house was empty and painters were coloring the interior for new tenants. Fortunately, Aharoni questioned the local people and soon discovered Eichmann's new address on Garibaldi Street.

Harel chose himself to command the abduction, with Peter Malkin and Rafael "Rafi" Eitan as his seconds and three others to round out the Israeli portion of the team. Harel had earlier said that he wished to capture Adolf Hitler personally, but Eichmann would have to do in the end.

In a bizarre incident that took place while he was traveling to Argentina, an official called Harel's false name over the loudspeakers at a South American airport, asking him to come to the information desk. When Harel arrived, fearing someone had compromised his alias, he found another man already at the desk talking with the clerks there. By chance, Harel's randomly selected pseudonym was the same as the actual name of another man taking the same flight.

A coincidental diplomatic visit to Argentina scheduled for May 11, 1960 provided the "cover" for the operation. The visit, which originally had nothing to do with Eichmann, involved Israeli Foreign Minister Abba Eban traveling to Argentina to offer congratulations during that nation's 150th Independence Day celebration. The journey would be carried out on an Israeli El Al flight – the historic first Transatlantic flight of the new airline. Naturally, this diplomatic mission provided a superb opportunity to put the Israeli team within striking distance of Eichmann, and the El Al aircraft, with its all-Israeli crew, provided the means by which Eichmann could be smuggled out of the country under the very noses of the Argentine authorities.

The six Israeli members of the team traveled to Argentina in April 1960 to prepare for the diplomatic mission. With Harel, Eitan, and Malkin at the helm, the operation went more smoothly than the ludicrous photographic expedition had a few weeks earlier. The Mossad agents came at different times and by various routes, only meeting up once all four were safely in Argentina. There, several Argentine Jews willing to participate in the plan joined them. "There were four of them, all South American residents, fluent in Spanish, and thoroughly familiar with Argentina in general and Buenos Aires in particular, through frequent business or personal visits. Two were a couple by the name of Kornfeld, David, a successful young architect, and Hedda, a graduate in psychology and languages; one was Lubinsky, a middle-aged lawyer [...] and the fourth was Primo, a second-year engineering student." (Harel, 1975, 43).

Harel's team worked thoroughly, researching Eichmann's habits without betraying themselves clumsily as the earlier team had, and renting no less than seven safe houses. This number of safe houses gave them a place to take Eichmann regardless of where they seized him or what route of retreat from the abduction site they were obliged to take. Multiple safe houses also permitted them to move Eichmann to a secure location, if necessary, should the Argentinian police compromise one of the safe houses after the German's capture.

At the last minute, the Argentine government postponed the meeting with Foreign Minister Abba Eban to one week later, May 19th, 1960. Isser Harel cheerfully declared that this was an even better turn of events because the extra week would give the Mossad the chance to try to bag Josef Mengele also. The Israelis did not yet know that Mengele had flown the coop to Paraguay with the aid of Hans-Ulrich Rudel.

The Israeli team took an initial practice run shortly after their arrival and, to their astonishment, saw and followed Eichmann to his home on their first day. They soon learned the bus routes he took, his work schedule at the Mercedes-Benz factory, and where he walked while returning home from work each day. Incautiously for a fugitive, Eichmann never varied his routine or routes, making him a relatively easy target.

The team quickly decided that the interval during which Eichmann walked from the bus stop to his home was the best time to abduct him, as the area was usually not crowded and Eichmann typically walked alone. He arrived late, generally as dusk was falling, so a passing police officer or friend seemed less likely to intervene in the dim light.

Moreover, if the Mossad agents waited until Eichmann reached his home, complications might arise. The sturdy brick house could be difficult to break into, giving the German time to seize a firearm and kill some or all of his assailants. Vera Eichmann and the three older sons might also intervene, worsening the odds, and the Israelis also wished to avoid collateral damage that might spark a manhunt even from the rather indifferent Argentine police. Accidentally killing Vera and the boys in an exchange of gunfire – and perhaps Eichmann's daughter-in-law as well – was something the men also did not want to have on their conscience. A clean, simple abduction with no unnecessary casualties would mark them as decisively different from the cold-blooded mass murderer they were hunting.

Harel and his seconds set May 11, 1960 as the date when Eichmann's abduction would take place. The Mossad agents would then keep their prisoner hidden at a safe house until the El Al flight arrived on May 19. The team was exhausted by this point after making innumerable preparations for the abduction, but they still found time to practice "dry runs" of the attack on Eichmann, with one of their number playing the part of the SS man walking along an isolated road and the others practicing various methods of pulling up in their cars, leaping out, overpowering their target, and wrestling him into the back seat of a vehicle. This extensive practice would wind up paying dividends.

Another member of the team, Yosef Klein, investigated Ezeiza Airport with commendable thoroughness. He hinted strongly that El Al planned to begin regular flights, and that the airline would hire numerous local people. This made the airport officials very willing to allow the Israeli to tour and inspect the entire airport, including many areas normally off-limits to the public. Klein collected valuable information: "Klein was certain that Eichmann could not be brought onto the plane through the terminal building, even if he were concealed in a trunk or other contraption. There were too many customs and immigration officers, and with the heightened security from both the terrorist attacks and the anniversary celebrations, little escaped their attention. [...] When Klein visited the TransAer facilities that afternoon, he found the ideal spot." (Bascomb, 2009, 200-201).

TransAer, a private airline, ran the same Bristol Type 175 Britannia "Whispering Giant" turboprop airliners as El Al, so Klein persuaded the TransAer management to allow the Israeli jet to park at their hangar due to the ready availability of Type 175 spare parts. The hangar stood removed from the other facilities, making it much easier to smuggle a man on board.

The other Mossad preparations were just as meticulous. Shalom Dani set about making a fake Israeli passport for Eichmann. Slowly dying of heart problems at age 32, Dani offered the team forgery skills which had already enabled their smoothly anonymous arrival in Argentina. The team also mapped out and drove three separate routes to each of their seven hideouts, driving each route repeatedly until they could follow them easily by day or night. Just to be on the safe side, they leased three extra apartments, bringing the number of safe houses to 10, and they bought two more cars, sleek black models that could imitate embassy transport.

Peter Malkin observed Eichmann with a telescope, finding strange philosophical food for thought in seeing the SS man crawling around the floor of his house and playing with his youngest son exactly like any other father. He also investigated the neighborhood, counted the number of strides from the bus stop to Eichmann's house, and thoroughly surveyed the terrain surrounding the area where the abduction was to take place. This information, he reasoned, might prove invaluable if Eichmann ran away and tried to hide in the vicinity.

Isser Harel met with the Israeli ambassador, Arye Levavi, at a quiet restaurant and discussed the plan with him. Levavi agreed to help in whatever way he could, and Harel cautioned him about possible consequences and the preparations to take against them. Harel "recommended to the ambassador that some volunteers be assembled at the embassy beginning on May 10, in case the operation was exposed early and there were vigilante attacks on the embassy. He explained that Eichmann's sons were connected to radical, strongly anti-Semitic nationalist groups. Levavi said that he would see to it." (Bascomb, 2009, 207).

Finally, after weeks of intensive preparations, May 10th arrived. The Mossad had scheduled the abduction to occur the next day, so the team scouted the route from the abduction site to the chosen safe house to ensure no unexpected changes had occurred along it. Nonetheless, later that afternoon, fate almost put a stop to the plan, showing how simple chance can potentially defeat even the most intricate and well-practiced plans. "Yitzhak, the official tenant of the house, drove to the city to buy food [...] On his way back [...] he collided with another car and both vehicles were badly damaged – fortunately, both he and the other driver came out of the accident with only slight injuries. To avoid police intervention Yitzhak took all the blame on himself and asked the other man to give him an estimate of the damage to his car. Without any bargaining Yitzhak paid him the whole amount in cash." (Harel, 1975, 155-156).

The Israeli agents spent the early part of May 11, 1960 preparing their cars and the safe house. Doubts plagued Peter Malkin, at least, over whether Ricardo Klement was in fact Adolf Eichmann or whether they were about to mistakenly abduct an innocent man who had nothing to do with Hitler or the Final Solution. Harel deputed Malkin to actually grapple Eichmann at the moment of capture, and this caused the agent to add a pair of leather gloves to his equipment: "The gloves would of course help with the cold, but that is not the main reason I bought them. The thought of placing my bare hand over the mouth that had ordered the death of millions, of feeling the hot breath and the saliva on my skin, filled me with an overwhelming sense of revulsion." (Malkin, 1990, 183).

The men left their hideout at 6:45 p.m. into the gathering darkness of evening, and the Mossad team knew the drive would occupy approximately half an hour, leaving them 15 minutes to set up before Eichmann arrived. Their plan was to park their two cars and then feign working on the engine of one as if it had broken down. As they left the main part of Buenos Aires and swung onto the highway, lightning flashed through the gloom and a heavy roll of thunder shuddered in the air. No rain fell from the storm at that point, but intermittent flashes lit the way and thunder rumbled in their ears as the Mossad agents drove to capture one of history's worst mass murderers.

The men parked just 60 feet from Eichmann's house and began to rummage in the engine compartment as if they were working on the engine. The lightning drew closer and the cracks of thunder were sharper as the evening light turned to a strange, surreal coppery shade under the wings of the approaching thunderstorm.

The time of Eichmann's arrival came and passed; for the first time in weeks, Eichmann failed to be punctual to the minute. The Mossad men feared he had caught wind of their plot and fled, but they waited. Finally, almost 40 minutes late, Eichmann's bus, the 203, appeared in the distance. At that moment, a young Argentinian man on a bicycle approached, smiling and waving, to help the men with their "broken-down" car. A quick-thinking Israeli slammed down the hood of the car and slapped his fellows on the back as if to congratulate them for fixing the vehicle, causing the young man to believe they had just successfully completed their repair. The youth called out something in Spanish with another smile, waved, and sped off down the road on his bicycle.

Finally, the Mossad agents saw their prey approaching. Strong, cold winds blowing ahead of the thunderstorm caused the German to turn up his collar and thrust his hands deep into his pockets, ignoring the men apparently working on a car engine directly ahead. It was at that moment that Peter Malkin walked forward to meet Eichmann. "'Un momentito, senor.' The simple sentence I had been practicing for weeks. He stopped. Behind black-rimmed glasses, his eyes met mine. He took a step backward. I leapt at him, grabbing for his right hand. We fell hard to the ground and tumbled into the shallow ditch alongside the walkway. I was on my back in a couple inches of mud, holding him with all my strength, one hand around his throat." (Malkin, 1990, 187).

Malkin lurched to his feet and released his grip on Eichmann's throat for an instant. The German screamed piercingly, an "animal" sound according to Malkin, who immediately squeezed his windpipe again. The SS man struggled furiously but Malkin was powerful, and two other Mossad agents dashed forward to grab Eichmann. The German was bundled into a car, blindfolded with taped-over goggles, and handcuffed. The Jews told Eichmann they would kill him if he screamed again, after which Malkin took his hand off the SS lieutenant colonel's mouth. Eichmann remained silent as the men scrambled into their cars and drove away.

The men experienced one bad moment on the way to the safe house when the backup car went astray on Route 202. However, only a few minutes passed before the two carloads of Mossad agents found one another again and drove on to their destination. There, the men brought Eichmann to the prison room they had prepared. Though obviously terrified, he initially denied being Eichmann. It was only when the Mossad agents examined him and found the scar in his armpit (where he had cut away his SS brand many years before) and confronted him with his SS number – 45326 – that the bony, decrepit man admitted who he was: "'Ich bin Adolf Eichmann,' he answered. After a pause, he added wearily but almost with relief: 'I know

I'm in the hands of Jews. I am resigned to my fate.'" (Levy, 2002, 153).

The architect of the Final Solution, once a dangerous man familiar with weapons and unarmed fighting techniques, was a feeble, emaciated wreck when captured. Despite knowing he was a hunted man, Eichmann was unarmed, with the only possession in his pockets a small flashlight. On the first day, he refused food, but after that, he entered a mode of strange compliance, which he followed even when it caused him great discomfort. For example, he asked permission to use the toilet, and once seated, he asked permission to begin defecating. He apologized profusely at each sound produced, and at the end he asked permission to use toilet paper to wipe himself. The men guarding him were initially astonished, then amused, and finally annoyed by this bizarre deference.

Once his initial terror was over, Eichmann began to talk constantly to his captors, focusing on his chief interest: himself. He explained that his work with the mass murder of the Holocaust was only work he had been forced to by circumstance, and that it was truly not his fault. No matter what twists of logic and subtlety Eichmann used, however, he never concealed his still iron-firm loyalty to Hitler, using the phrase "The Fuhrer was infallible!" to deflect any criticism of his idol.

The Mossad men moved their prisoner once while they waited for the El Al flight to arrive, fearing that some activity near the first safe house indicated interest in their prisoner. In the meantime, the search for Eichmann was not particularly thorough or energetic: "Vera Eichmann waited three days before approaching anyone about her missing husband. She made the round of hospitals and morgues while her sons contacted Nazi welfare and Argentine fascist organizations, none of which paid much heed to an obscure émigré named Klement who seemed to have left his family. When the police finally were notified, their inquiries, too, were strictly routine." (Levy, 2002, 153).

The wait for the El Al airliner's arrival stretched the nerves of Isser Harel and his men, but nothing happened during the days of waiting. Eichmann talked constantly when awake, ate, exercised, and even wrote a short statement. The Mossad men bided their time, feeling a mix of emotions ranging from pure hate to a state approaching detached pity. The apparent normality and vulnerability of the middle-aged, infirm man in their hands jarred strangely against the terrible image of the young Eichmann in his crisp uniform, brandishing a pistol or, in the nightmares of Wiesenthal, a bullwhip as he drove millions to their deaths.

Eichmann's terror and compliance are explicable in more terms than personal cowardice. He admitted after several days that he was terrified the Mossad men would torture and kill his wife and children before leaving. Startled at the notion, they assured him they had no intention to do so, but Eichmann refused to believe them and periodically begged them not to kill his children. The idea that anyone would refrain from committing a cruelty that it was in their power to inflict was apparently so alien to him that he could not accept it, even when it worked to his advantage.

Harel put the plan's final phase into operation when the El Al flight arrived on May 19. Despite keen disappointment at Josef Mengele's escape, which was confirmed by Eichmann's statements, he retained his professional focus and concentrated on getting his prisoner out of the country. Harel gave Avraham Shalom the task of arranging the actual extraction, and the day before the aircraft's arrival, Peter Malkin applied a trial run makeup to Eichmann's face, filling in wrinkles and making him appear to be a much younger man. Eichmann put on an El Al uniform, which included a peaked cap not unlike his SS cap, and when the men allowed the prisoner to look at himself in a mirror, the result astounded his captors; Eichmann drew himself up to attention, radiating an air of authority, and he adjusted the peaked cap precisely before declaring, "Ist gut. Ist wunderbar." He began to strut up and down the room, face full of belligerence and cold pride, closely resembling his younger portrait and thoroughly unnerving his Mossad captors.

Despite the massive security arrangements, Shalom's plan to get Eichmann aboard the "Whispering Giant" went off flawlessly. A doctor gave Eichmann a soporific drug and splashed him with whiskey so he would appear inebriated. Bearing the passport of the fictional "George Doron," he was hustled aboard the aircraft on May 20 in the midst of the aircrew. The airliner lumbered off the ground, propellers whirring, and rose into the Argentine sky. It made only one stop on the way, taking on more fuel at the city of Dakar in Senegal. At around dawn on May 21, the airline coasted to a stop at Tel Aviv airfield, carrying Eichmann into Israeli captivity.

The Mossad unit in Argentina did not leave quite as easily. Their flight through Valparaiso was canceled due to a massive earthquake. In fact, the 1960 Valdivia Earthquake was the most powerful ever scientifically measured, killing 6,000 people, including 61 in Hilo, Hawaii due to a tsunami. This 9.5 moment magnitude scale shock damaged the Valparaiso airfield and forced the Mossad men to remain in Argentina for several days after their quarry was gone.

The world greeted news of Eichmann's abduction with astonishment, while the mood in Argentina was one of rage. Right-wing and fascist groups beat Jews, killed several, and threw improvised bombs at Jewish consulates, shops, and other buildings. The last known victim of these crimes was the Argentinian daughter of the owner of the safe house where the Mossad held Eichmann. The day after Eichmann's execution, fascist thugs kidnapped Graciela Narcisa Sirota, then just 19 years old, after which they raped her, tortured her viciously, and branded her breasts with swastikas before tossing her, alive but in great pain, onto the street near the safe house.

In contrast to these brutal events, the Israelis carried out Eichmann's arraignment and trial with civilized punctiliousness. In the ensuing months, Eichmann continued to claim that he was just following orders, and that he was an unimportant pencil pusher who had no real control over what happened under Hitler and Himmler. However, Eichmann's own tendency to talk too much helped seal his fate; while in exile, he had narrated an autobiography to his fellow exile Sassen, recorded on several hundred hours of tapes. The prosecution played these tapes in court, and on them, Eichmann's distinctive voice droned on and on, describing Jews as a disease in need of a cure, as a demonic influence on history, and that it was the duty of every good Aryan to wipe Jews out. Far from coming across as a bland administrator, Eichmann's own words depicted him as a strident anti-Semite who believed fervently in exterminating an entire people because of an absurd conspiracy theory.

In many respects, the Eichmann trial was not just a trial of one man but of anti-Semitism itself, and a global expose of the horrors of the Holocaust. Researchers presented and read thousands of original Third Reich documents, and hundreds of witnesses appeared for the prosecution, describing the imprisonment, torture, rape, mutilation, starvation, disease, and murder of millions of human beings in excruciating detail. "Most of them had no direct relation to Eichmann's doings, and in an ordinary trial their testimonies would have been disqualified due to lack of relevance. But their cries, their despair, the exposing of secrets they had carried inside them like malignant tumors—all those were much more important than the trial itself. They enabled the Israelis… to understand something that [had] until then remained out of the public eye: The power of the personal account over that of the official narrative." (Goldstein, 2012, 294).

Eichmann's fate was a foregone conclusion, but the trial proved to the world that he and the other leading Nazis deserved it. The trial documented the Holocaust so extensively that many people inclined to disbelieve it changed their minds. Denial of the six million murders became disreputable overnight as the endless scroll of accusations, letters, orders, photos, films, and other proofs unrolled before the eyes of the court and the world. With that, the horror and absurdity of anti-Semitism (and indeed all forms of racism) was laid bare in relentless detail. The skeletons in history's closet, the centuries of furtive oppression and open pogroms, were confronted at last. "James Parkes, an Anglican priest and expert on early Christianity, attended the Eichmann trial. In Parkes's view, the trial revealed that 'there is an unbroken chain which goes back from Hitler's death camps to the denunciations of [Jews by] the early Church.' Not long after the trial ended, the Protestant World Council of Churches issued a document condemning antisemitism and stating that contemporary Jews were in no way responsible for the death of Jesus." (Goldstein, 2012, 293).

The trial concluded on December 1, 1961 with the judges sentencing Eichmann to death.

While listening to the judgment, Eichmann showed signs of panic, sweating profusely as he jerked about in his seat and looking around frantically in all directions as if seeking a route of escape. The SS man's fate was the only death sentence ever issued in Israel from its founding to the present day. Eichmann naturally appealed the judgment, but in light of the damning evidence accumulated against him, the Israelis denied this plea on May 29, 1962. The judges scheduled Eichmann for execution by hanging at the stroke of midnight two days later.

As he awaited his execution on May 31, 1962, Eichmann consumed half a bottle of white wine, smoked several cigarettes, and wrote a letter to his family. He walked to the execution room calmly, moving so quickly that he forced his guards to hurry to keep up. Since the state of Israel had no execution facilities, one had been hastily put together to accommodate the nation's first and last capital offender.

Eichmann refused a hood, and though he was pale, he retained his composure. As midnight approached, he stated, "Long live Germany! Long live Argentina! Long live Austria! These are the three nations I am most connected with and shall not forget. I greet my wife, my family, and my friends. I am ready." He paused for a moment and then addressed his executioners directly with a cold smile: "Gentlemen, we shall meet again soon, as is the fate of all men." Then he added, "I have believed in God all my life. I die believing in God."

The trapdoor snapped open, and Eichmann fell 10 feet. Unlike the unfortunate victims whom his SS men had hanged with their toes just touching the ground in Auschwitz and Treblinka so that they could struggle in agony and fear for a time before being strangled to death, Eichmann's death was instantaneous as his neck snapped.

To date, Eichmann is the only individual to receive the death sentence in Israel's history.

Chapter 8: The Six-Day War

Perhaps buoyed by the success with Eichmann, Harel's fervor for vengeance led to the disgrace of Israeli intelligence when he "became obsessed with the Holocaust." In time, he launched a campaign of murderous intimidation against a team of German scientists whom he suspected were building rockets for the Egyptians to use against Israel.[39] According to historian George Lavy, Egyptian President Gamal Abdel Nasser was certainly driving an Egyptian rocket program, but it was more in support of the objective to keep up with Israel's rocket technology while maintaining Egypt's Cold War policy of non-alignment with the United States and the Soviet Union. Their goal was to develop their military industry, rather than an offensive campaign against Israel.[40]

At the same time, Ben-Gurion was proud of Israel's improved relations with West Germany. In spite of Egypt's public rocket tests, which worried the world in 1962, West Germany continued paying reparations while covertly supplying arms to

Israel, thus maintaining what some consider an overall healthy relationship with their former enemy.[41] Under Harel's leadership, Mossad obtained a document written by Wolfgang Pilz, a German scientist, detailing weak evidence that the rocket factory was being prepared for the development of chemical, biological, and gas-filled warheads for the rockets.

Convinced that Mossad had no time to find stronger evidence, Harel launched "Operation Damocles," a series of subversive operations against German and Egyptian scientists. He planted stories about the sinister weapons to gain support from the Israeli population and directed his teams to execute letter bomb attacks and abduct Egyptian scientists and their families. When confronted about these brutal tactics, Harel replied, "There are people who are marked to die."[42]

The public heard of several mysterious casualties, abductions, and the deaths of German and Egyptian scientists and their family members and coworkers before the arrest of two Mossad agents, Joseph Ben-

Gal and Otto Joklik, in Switzerland. The agents were arrested for threatening Heidi Goercke, the daughter of a West German electronic guidance expert working at a factory Mossad suspected of helping Israel's enemies. The agents were charged with coercion and illegal operation on behalf of a foreign state, leading to investigations tying them to abductions and assassination attempts.

All of this caused a public scandal for Israel, which publicly denied the claims and asserted its agents used only methods of "peaceful persuasion."[43] Foreign Minister Golda Meir had worked hard with other Israeli diplomats to build relations between West Germany and Israel, so they were understandably worried about the consequences for Israel's relations with West Germany and demanded Mossad halt such operations. Ben-Gurion insisted Harel resign as chief of Mossad, and that led to a wave of resignations in protest by those loyal to Harel within the intelligence institution. Eventually, the scandal drove Ben-Gurion to resign as prime minister in

January 1963,[44] and Western countries lost considerable trust in Israel. All were dismayed in 1967 when Egypt began purchasing Scud B rockets from the Soviet Union.

Golda Meir

Despite losing the 1948 war, Arab nations throughout the Middle East had still refused to recognize Israel's right to exist. After the Suez Canal War, Egyptian leader Gamal Abdel Nasser envisioned creating a unified Arab world, commonly referred to as pan-Arabism. Nasser was the consummate pan-Arab leader in the 1960s, positioning himself as the leader of the Arab world through increasing incitement against Israel with rhetoric.

Israel found itself in possession of more land after 1948 than envisioned by the U.N. Partition Plan, but the Green Line still left it less than 10 miles wide in some positions. In the summer of 1967, the armies of Jordan and Syria mobilized near Israel's borders, while Egypt's army mobilized in the Sinai Peninsula just west of the Gaza Strip.

Combined, the Arab armies numbered over 200,000 soldiers.

In 1966, with Soviet encouragement, Nasser brokered on behalf of Egypt a mutual defense pact with Syria, committing either territory to the defense of the other in the case of Israeli aggression.

All of this contributed to a growing sense of vulnerability in Israel, but there were other peripheral issues that also helped raise diplomatic tensions in the region. One such was the Arab League's plans to divert the water of the Jordan River away from Israel, and no secret was made of the fact that this would be undertaken as part of a wider destabilization effort. On April 7, 1967, a clash took place between Syrian and Israeli forces that began with an artillery duel and ended in an air battle in which six Syrian MiG- 21s were shot down.

In May 1967, an erroneous and perhaps deliberately destabilizing Soviet intelligence report was made available to Egyptian intelligence, indicating a large-scale Israeli troop build-up massing on Israel's northern border in preparation to attack Syria. The Israelis denied this and offered diplomatic guarantees, but Nasser began his own force build-up in the Sinai. Four Egyptian brigades were deployed on the peninsula, and Nasser ordered the 3,400 strong United Nations peacekeeping force to vacate their positions on Israel's southern border. The UN Emergency Force, or UNEF, had been established in the region after the 1956 Sinai/Suez conflict, and United Nations Secretary-General, U Thant, complied with this directive with very little, if any protest. He bypassed the General Assembly, which was contrary to protocol at the very least.

This established a very dangerous precedent on the peninsula, and on the part of Egypt, it certainly was difficult to see it as anything less than an unambiguous provocation. Egyptian forces were now in a position to mobilize against Israel without hindrance in the Sinai, and by having ordered the United Nations around, Nasser's prestige within the Arab League was considerably enhanced.

Meanwhile, Israel had established a number of clear criteria under which it would consider itself at war, or under the threat of war from its neighbors. These included the blockading of the Straits of Tiran, which would effectively shut the Israeli Port of Eilat, on the Gulf of Aqaba, off from international shipping; the deployment of Iraqi troops into Jordan; the signing of an Egyptian/Jordanian defense agreement; and the withdrawal of the UN emergency force. The latter's withdrawal, and the alacrity with which it was undertaken, was certainly seen by Israel as a large measure of Egypt's seriousness, but on May 22, 1967, Nasser went further by blockading the Straits of Tiran to Israeli shipping. At the very least, this was a violation of international law, and the Israeli defense establishment began to take the threat of war very seriously indeed.

United States President Lyndon B. Johnson, later commenting on events as they unfolded during that tense spring of 1967, observed, "If a single act of folly was more responsible for this explosion than any other, it was the arbitrary and dangerous announced decision that the Straits of Tiran would be closed." Nonetheless, the White

House urged restraint, offering the assistance of an international flotilla, Operation Red Sea Regatta, to challenge it, but in the end, largely thanks to American and Soviet naval sparring in the Mediterranean, this initiative never got off the ground.

President Johnson

Despite having raised tensions with flawed and largely unverified intelligence reports, the Soviet position was initially ambiguous, and no overt encouragement was expressed towards Egypt over the closure of the Straits of Tiran. A Pravda article that appeared three days after the closure was limited to observing that Israel had not enjoyed a right of access to the Gulf of Aqaba prior to 1956, and so, therefore, she had no supportable claim to access now. This was followed on May 23 by an official Soviet dispatch that repeated accusations that Israel was preparing for an attack against Syria, warning that the result of such an action would not only be a united and dramatic Arab response but also that "strong opposition" might be expected from the

Soviet Union and all other peace-loving states. In fact, Soviet support for the Arabs remained equivocal throughout, and the only clear commitment was an undertaking to offer direct Soviet support to the Arabs only if direct U.S. support was offered to Israel.

In the wake of Nasser's actions, Israeli Prime Minister Levi Eshkol issued an official statement warning that Egyptian interference with Israeli shipping would be regarded as an act of aggression. Despite this, Eshkol resisted the hawks in both his government and defense establishment for several weeks, holding out against a preemptive strike without expressed American support, and certainly against the risk of being internationally judged as being the aggressor.

Eshkol

Nasser, however, maintained a steady outflow of aggressive rhetoric. In a speech delivered on May 26, he stated, "Recently we have felt strong enough that if we enter a battle with Israel, with God's help, we could triumph. On this basis we decided to take actual steps...taking over Sharm ash-Shaykh...meant that we were ready to enter a general war with Israel...and our objective would be to destroy Israel."

A few days later, further military defense pacts were signed between Egypt, Jordan and Iraq, theoretically unifying the forces of all three against Israel, and adding to a definitive breach of the conditions for war that Israel had already spelled out. King Hussein of Jordan, generally the least belligerent of the Arab "frontline" members, marked the moment with the following observation: "All of the Arab armies now surround Israel. The UAR, Iraq, Syria, Jordan, Yemen, Lebanon, Algeria, Sudan, and Kuwait...there is no difference between one Arab people and another, no difference between one Arab army and another."

Nasser and King Hussein of Jordan

This sort of talk, at least in the context of local military realities, was probably not to be taken very seriously since Arab unity had remained throughout Israel's short existence more of a talking point than a strategic reality. The fact nonetheless remained, however, that Israel, with a small army mostly comprised of citizen reserves, was facing the combined threat of several Arab nations, each committed to the single objective of its destruction. At that point, the Israeli Defense Force, while confident that victory was possible, was not yet quite so convinced of its tactical superiority as to believe that defeat was impossible.

The ongoing mobilization of Egyptian forces in the Sinai was the source of continuing anxiety in Tel Aviv, and the sort of threatening media and public language emanating from Egypt, from the Syrian defense establishment, and from the ranks of the PLO, all seemed to confirm a united and imminent Arab threat.

Israeli Prime Minister Levi Eshkol eventually succumbed to political and public pressure. Seeing the writing on the wall, on June 5, 1967, he relinquished the portfolio of Minister of Defense, which he held, to Moshe Dayan, signalling that war had become inevitable.

Dayan

In 1967, the Israeli Air Force consisted of about 260 combat aircraft (mostly French/Dassault Aviation), although figures in this regard vary depending on the source. Combined Arab air forces consisted of some 341 Egyptian, 90 Syrian, and 18 Jordanian combat aircraft, most of which were Soviet-supplied (although the Jordanians did operate a flight of British Hawker Hunters). Bearing this in mind, Israeli defence planners considered the Egyptian long-range bomber fleet, and the prior deployment of Egyptian forces in the Sinai, as the clearest and most imminent threat.

Israeli intelligence, a growing force among international intelligence agencies, had established that the Arabs in general, and Egypt in particular, were poorly prepared for war. There were many reasons for this, but in the case of Egypt, the politicization of the army and the politicization of war undermined both. Nasser, for example, was suspicious of the educated elite of his nation, and he avoided the involvement in the military of any element potentially hostile to him, fearing a potential coup. This tended to result in a lower quality of junior and mid-level command, and a lower technical appreciation of sophisticated weapons that now characterized the battlefield.

The Egyptian operational plan in the Sinai was called Operation Kahir, and until the last minute, Nasser tampered with it and changed it. This would result in considerable confusion when fighting broke out, and it contributed to a general lack of coordination at the launch of the campaign between senior and operational commanders, and between operational commanders and men in the field.

The Egyptian defense infrastructure was also known to be generally poor, and despite large numbers of combat aircraft, very few facilities such as underground revetments and hardened shelters, had been introduced to the main Egyptian Air Force bases. Electronic air defenses were also out of action, for reasons of internal security (Nasser did not trust his generals), which further opened up the skies for attack. Egyptian aircraft were most vulnerable on the ground, and it was there that the Israelis hit them.

Operation Focus (Moked) was launched at precisely 07h45 on Monday, June 5, 1967. The essence of the Israeli plan was simply to direct its entire air offensive capacity (just 12 aircraft were held back to defend Israeli airfields) to deal with Egyptian aircraft before the Syrians or the Jordanians had time to intervene, after which Israel would deal with each one in turn. Operation Focus was a highly coordinated, precisely timed series of attacks that initially targeted 10 Egyptian airfields in the first wave, and 9 more on the second. These attacks were intended to destroy the Egyptian Air Force while it was still on the ground.

The time of the first launch – 07h45 – was extremely important for four reasons. At that hour, the Egyptians had already flown their first morning combat patrols, so they were back on the ground at breakfast. Moreover, on a Monday morning, most Egyptian high ranking officers would either be at home or en route to work, taking them out of the picture during the vital moments of the attack. The timing also allowed the IAF pilots earmarked for the attack to enjoy a full night's sleep before the commencement of what would be a long and punishing day. Lastly, the normally heavy morning mist and fog over the combat zone would have lifted by then, allowing for better target acquisition.

The initial attack lasted 80 minutes, comprising eight waves of four aircraft each. The planes spent about 10 minutes over the target area, followed typically less than three minutes later by the next. After the initial 80 minute assault, the Egyptians were given just 10 minutes to catch their breath before the second 80 minute attack was launched. By noon, a total of 19 Egyptian airfields had been comprehensively targeted in the Sinai, the Suez Canal Zone, in and around Cairo, up the Nile Valley, and on the west bank of the Red Sea. In those first three hours, the Egyptian Air Force lost 300 of its 340 aircraft, including its entire fleet of Soviet-supplied TU-16 long-range bombers and almost all of its combat aircraft.

A picture of destroyed Egyptian planes on the ground

Israeli intelligence was also able to pinpoint only operationally significant targets, which avoided wasted time, while finely rehearsed turnarounds of 10-12 minutes ensured that Israeli aircraft were applied to maximum effect.

At 08h10 on June 5, 1967, the Israel Broadcasting Authority aired an Israeli Defense Force communique. "Since the early hours of this morning," it read, "heavy fighting has been taking place on the southern front between Egyptian armored and aerial forces, which moved against Israel, and our forces, which went into action to check them." This was followed up a little over two hours later by a publicly aired message to the armed forces of Israel, released by Israeli Minister of Defense Moshi Dayan in his first day in office. "We have no aims of conquest," was Dayan' simple message. "Our only aim is to frustrate the attempt of the Arab armies to conquer our country, and to sever and crush the ring of blockade and aggression which has been created around us."

By then, the Israeli Air Force had been in action over the skies of Egypt since 07h45 that morning, and as a consequence, almost the entire Egyptian Air Force lay smoldering on the tarmacs of various forward Egyptian airbases. Having neutralized Egypt's air strike potential in a matter of hours, the IAF then began to turn its attention to Jordan, Iraq and Syria, as IDF ground forces, back in the Sinai, moved in to take care of the more punishing business of destroying Egyptian ground forces.

These public protestations, declaring that Israel desired only peace and would initiate no aggressive action against any neighbor, rang more than a little hollow in the face of all of this, but in the context of Israeli national survival, it had been agreed that offense was defense. The only rational defensive doctrine, bearing in mind Israel's extreme vulnerability, was to take the war to the Arabs. Only in this way could the comparatively diminutive Israeli armed forces have any hope of victory.

Over the next six days, the Israelis overwhelmed the Egyptians in the west, destroying thousands of tanks and capturing the Gaza Strip and the entire Sinai Peninsula. At the same time, Israel drove the Jordanians out of Jerusalem and the West Bank, and it captured the Golan Heights from Syria near the border of Lebanon. In the span of a week, Israel had tripled the size of the lands it controlled. Israel had gone from less than 10 miles wide in some spots to over 200 miles wide from the Sinai Peninsula to the West Bank. Israel also unified Jerusalem.

The results of the Six Day War created several issues that have still not been resolved in the Middle East. Israel now found itself in possession of territories that were the home of over a million Arabs. Of these territories, Israel officially annexed only East Jerusalem and the Golan Heights, leaving the inhabitants of the West Bank, Sinai Peninsula, and Gaza Strip in limbo regarding citizenship status.

Despite attempts to create peace, the Arab nations refused to recognize Israel, and

Israel refused to withdraw from any of the land it captured in 1967. After conquering the territories, Israel began encouraging Jewish settlement in the new territories. In the 1970s, more than 10,000 Jews moved into the West Bank, Gaza Strip, Golan Heights, East Jerusalem, and the Sinai Peninsula, a figure that grew to over 100,000 by the early '80s and is now over 500,000 today. Some in Israel note that Jewish settlements in 1967 had simply reestablished Jewish communities in places they had lived prior to 1948, including Jerusalem, Hebron, and Gush Etzion, as well as Gaza City in the Gaza Strip. They also argue that the legal status of the territories was never officially determined due to the Palestinian rejection of the U.N. Partition Plan. Still others assert that Israel's settlements do not breach international law or the Geneva Convention because it fought the Six Day War in self-defense and did not forcibly transfer civilian populations onto occupied territories. However, despite those arguments, the vast majority of the world considers Jewish settlements on land captured by Israel in 1967 to be illegal, including the United Nations, the International Court of Justice, and the international community.

The war also illustrated the degree to which Mossad was critical to the IDF in the late 1960s, as well as the controversial nature of how Mossad applied intelligence. Pro-Israel historians lauded Eli Cohen as a hero during this conflict for his penetration of the Syrian leadership, as Cohen gathered intelligence on Syrian battle positions and warned leaders of the IDF that Syria had built extensive defensive fortifications in depths of up to 50 feet structured in a way that was compatible to France's Maginot Line during World War II.[45] Using the information provided by Cohen on the location and armaments at these fortifications, IDF leaders were able to create a strategy maximizing close combat rather than open combat, allowing their Uzi-armed forces to overcome the Syrian forces armed with the heavier AK-47. Historian Ian Black credits Cohen's contribution as the key enabler of the Israelis' capture of the Golan Heights.[46]

The war also demonstrated how the Mossad had aligned itself with the United States. For instance, in late May 1967, Meir Amit, the head of Mossad, traveled to Washington in disguise and on a false passport. Years later, in an interview with Amit, the retired spy said he had told Secretary of Defense Robert McNamara, "I'm going to recommend war." In response, McNamara allegedly asked, "How long?" He also asked, "How many casualties?" Amit stated that when he told him there would be fewer than 6,000 casualties, which was the number of Israel's War of Independence, McNamara is said to have replied, "I read you loud and clear."[47]

President Johnson flashed an "amber light" to Amit, signaling that the United States would not engage in activities of restraint or retaliation if Israel took an aggressive stance in anticipation of the need to defend their territory.[48] Similarly, the argument has been made that the Soviet Union manipulated Egyptian and Israeli intelligence to precipitate the war, although its primary alignment was with Egypt at this time.[49]

Chapter 9: Wrath of God

Following the Six-Day War, things did not get more secure in the Middle East, and Mossad seems to have adapted increasingly brutal methods to achieve objectives. Accounts of the intelligence community refer to the 1970s as "the war of spooks" because there was an escalation of Mossad officers under diplomatic cover going abroad and recruiting unprecedented numbers of informants from Fatah and other Palestinian groups. Inevitably, these operations did not always end well, such as when Baruch Cohen, a Shin Bet Arabic speaker on temporary assignment, was shot in a Madrid cafe by his own agent.[50] These kinds of operations would go a long way in making the Mossad legendary in some circles and infamous in others.

At 10:00 a.m. on September 12, 1972, Prime Minister Golda Meir appeared before a special session of the Knesset, the Israeli parliament. Wasting no time, the austere, chain-smoking grandmother addressed a full house of 120 members. "I want to share my plans with you," she said. 'I've decided to pursue each and every one of them. Not one of the people involved in any way will be walking around on this earth for much longer. We will chase them to the last."

These determined and resolute words were spoken in reference to the surviving operatives and planners of one of the most audacious terrorist attacks mounted against Israel since the founding of the nation in 1948. A week earlier, on September 5, 1972, 8 Palestinian terrorists belonging to the Black September faction of the Palestine Liberation Organization (PLO) entered the Olympic Village in Munich, West Germany, and took 11 Israeli athletes and team members hostage. After a lengthy standoff and a bungled rescue operation, all 11 were killed.

Black September was a shadowy and loosely configured organization, the nature and structure of which has been disputed by historians and journalists since it first appeared in 1972. It is generally regarded as a splinter group of Fatah, although some sources claim that it was simply a smokescreen used by Fatah to avoid direct complicity in certain operations. Other sources claim that it represented an ideological and tactical break from the traditional Fedayeen, with a more international complexion to its organization and structure. Either way, it was an extremist group shut down by the PLO in September 1973, on the anniversary of its creation, ostensibly because of a withdrawal of the PLO from terrorist operations abroad.

The key element of Golda Meir's speech was the sense of outrage felt by the Israeli people against an act that transgressed both the essential principles of the Olympic Games and the unwritten charter of the Israeli people, drawn up over less than three decades of uncertain existence. Israel was founded on little more than determination and religious and social cohesion, forged in a crucible of war against unequal odds and the fanatical resolve of all of its neighbors to see it destroyed. While today Israel is one of the most divisive political subjects across the world, the Munich Massacre and the Israeli operations in response all came about entirely because of the emotional power inherent in the Israeli-Arab conflict.

Prime Minister Meir's comments to the Knesset on September 12, 1972, were emotional and reactionary, but they absolutely spoke for a military and security establishment already digesting the lessons of Munich. The first response was an operation to hit the Palestinians and those who supported them with a punitive conventional attack. This was immediate and extremely aggressive, and it amounted to a massive series of precision air raids against all and any suspected terrorist camps from southern Lebanon to northern Jordan, including western Syria. It was successful, and even in the light of the Arab propensity for propaganda, it was difficult for the various enemies of Israel to claim that the targets had not been legitimate. More than a triumph of Israeli conventional capacity, this was a triumph of Israeli intelligence.

These initial attacks began almost immediately, commencing on September 9 and lasting for 24-hours. The ferocity of this response shocked not only the Arab states targeted and the guerrilla groups involved, but the international community too. Press analysis arrived at the conclusion, the very conclusion that Israel sought to provoke, that the future Israeli response to terror attacks against its citizens would be an "eye for an eye." This was confirmed in many Israeli speeches and utterances in the aftermath of the massacre. Meir herself, angered by the affair, issued numerous threats, most of which were backed up by military action. As General Aharon Yariv put it, "We had no choice. We had to make them stop, and there was no other way ... we are not very proud about it. But it was a question of sheer necessity. We went back to the old biblical rule of an eye for an eye ... I approach these problems not from a moral point of view, but, hard as it may sound, from a cost-benefit point of view. If I'm very hard-headed, I can say, what is the political benefit in killing this person? Will it bring us nearer to peace? Will it bring us nearer to an understanding with the Palestinians or not? In most cases I don't think it will. But in the case of Black

September we had no other choice and it worked. Is it morally acceptable? One can debate that question. Is it politically vital? It was."

Eventually, the response to the events in Munich gave way to Operation Wrath of God, which, as the name makes clear, aimed for a retaliation greater than anything ever before seen. Prime Minister Meir authorized the formation of a top-secret counterterrorism committee – Committee X – headed by General Yariv, ex-military attaché to Washington and ex-head of Aman, the Israeli military intelligence agency. A pedigreed senior military officer, Yariv was appointed to the position of Prime Minister's Advisor on Counterterrorism. Committee X was, in practical terms, an ad hoc, secret, closed tribunal formulated to examine and pass judgment of life or death on individuals and groups identified as being either connected to the planning and execution of the Munich operation, or in some other way affiliated with the PLO and Black September.

Yariv

Israeli journalist Yoel Marcus, in a report published in the Israeli newspaper Har'aretz on June 10, 1986, noted, "The panel (Committee X) concluded that the most effective means to make a clear statement that Israel would not tolerate terrorist activity was to authorize the assassination of any Black September terrorists involved in the Munich incident. This directive included any individual identified as either directly or indirectly involved in the planning or the execution of the assault on the Israeli athletes in Munich."

Committee X assigned the Mossad the task of implementing its directives, under the clear mandate to kill the Black September operatives, members, and affiliates, and not to capture and prosecute them. Assassination was the mandate of the Committee, and the objective was to counter terror with terror.

Mossad Chief Zvi Zamir appointed senior agent Michael Harari to oversee the development of special covert action teams. Harari worked in conjunction with a Mossad operations officer Abraham Gehmer, who worked under official cover as the First Secretary of the Israeli Embassy in Paris.[51] The Mossad established Paris as its regional base for European operations.

Shay Aloni's picture of Zvi Zamir

Even as plans were being put together for this operation, a more orthodox commando operation mounted to deal with three Back September operatives took place in Lebanon in April 1973. This was Operation Spring of Youth. That February, Israeli intelligence received confirmation of the whereabouts of three senior PLO leaders in Beirut. These were Muhammad Youssef al-Najjar (Abu Youssef), an operations leader in Black September; Kamal Adwan, a PLO chief of operations; and Kamal Nasser, PLO spokesman and member of the PLO Executive Committee. This information, including photographs and addresses, was passed on to Ehud Barak, who was then commander of the storied Sayeret Matkal, also known as General Staff Reconnaissance Unit 269. It was Barak and the Sayeret Matkal who planned and executed Operation Isotope, the successful rescue of hostages aboard Sabena Flight 571 in May 1972.

Barak

The planning of Operation Spring of Youth, as it was eventually finalized, was to drop Israeli operatives from navy ships, reach the beaches of Beirut in inflatable dinghies, and then, disguised as tourists (some, including Barak himself, posed as women), enter the city, target the individuals in their respective apartment buildings, and then leave by the same means. Detailed planning and training took place in apartment buildings in Tel Aviv that were similar in design to those that would be targeted.

The operation took place on April 9, 1973. That day, Israeli agents were waiting on shore with three cars, and the commandos were driven to their targets. While members stood guard outside the buildings, which were opposite one another, commandoes entered, blew out the doors, entered the apartments and gunned down the three targets, gathering what documents and other intelligence they could.

These assassinations were clinical, but they were also high profile, and in the case of Muhammad Youssef al-Najjar, his wife was also killed in the shootout. In the street below, the backup team was engaged in a firefight against local gendarmes and PLO response teams. Two Lebanese policemen were killed in that fighting. The Israelis then boarded their vehicles and returned to the beach. There they were observed by a Lebanese military armored troop carrier that did not attempt to engage them.

As this operation was taking place, 14 Israeli commandos, mainly paratroopers from Sayeret Tzanhanim, another storied Israeli commando unit, were engaged in heavy action at another location in Beirut against militants of the PFLP. Although dozens of PFLP fighters were killed, the Israeli unit became bogged down, and it eventually had to be extracted by helicopter.

Two secondary actions dealing with Fatah's headquarters in Beirut and a small Fatah explosives workshop, along with the PLO's main vehicle workshop in Sidon, were also successful.

Given how the operation went, Barak and his team of commandos could reflect on the beginnings of a counterterrorism strategy that would influence future special forces training and indoctrination in most of the major military formations of the world.

In the meantime, Operation Wrath of God was rolled out, and heading the list of those targeted for special treatment were those Black September operatives perceived to be responsible for the Munich attack. It was also agreed that the killings of those thus identified must be dramatic, and although plausible deniability would always be deployed, there would never be any doubt who was behind the operations.

According to anecdotal reporting of the affair, Meir was initially uncomfortable with the extrajudicial nature of the proposed operation and the possible political ramifications of such an open policy of political assassination. Her mind, however, was changed by the hijacking on October 29, 1972, of Lufthansa Flight 615, en route from Damascus to Frankfurt. Departing from a stopover in Beirut, two Arab passengers threatened to blow up the aircraft if the surviving members of the Black September group responsible for the Munich massacre, then being held in German prisons, were not released. The West German authorities acceded to these demands, and the three were flown to Zagreb in the former Yugoslavia, where they were handed over to the hijackers. The aircraft then refueled and flew to Tripoli, where the exchange was made and the hostages were released.

The reaction in the Arab world was jubilant, and the three were feted, were allowed to deliver a press conference, and generally celebrated their release. Thereafter they were permitted to remain at liberty in Libya, under the protection of Libyan leader Muammar Gaddafi. The German government congratulated itself in somewhat subdued tones, while the Israeli government loudly condemned what it considered an abject capitulation to terror. Whatever reservations the Israeli prime minister had over the implementation of a program of assassination vanished, and the three surviving Black September operatives

– Jamal Al-Gashey, Adnan Al-Gashey, and Mohammed Safady – were placed immediately in the crosshairs of Committee X.

The fate of all three of these men remains clouded by official secrecy, but it is generally believed that Adnan Al-Gashey and Mohammed Safady were both assassinated by Mossad. Authoritative reports and subsequent analysis present the possibility that Adnan Al-Gashey died of heart failure in Dubai sometime in the late 1970s, possibly in 1978 or 1979. The same source claims that Mohammed Safady was killed in an unrelated assassination conducted by Christian Phalangists in Lebanon in the early 1980s.[52] The latter account could possibly be true, but the former seems improbable, bearing in mind that Adnan Al-Gashey's age at the time would have been about 30. In the Academy Award-winning documentary, One Day in September, released in 2000, it is claimed that both Adnan Al-Gashey and Mohammad Safady were targeted and killed by Israeli agents.

Jamal Al-Gashey remained in hiding, spending some time in the United States and Canada. In fact, he made a brief appearance in the documentary mentioned above. Believing, with some justification that he was still on the Israeli hit list, his face was blurred and he wore dark glasses and a hat.

Perhaps the most interesting revelation to come from this, if it is indeed true, is that the hijacking of Lufthansa Flight 615 was orchestrated by the German government in order to rid itself of the potential embarrassment of a trial. German failures during the episode remained a source of deep embarrassment, and details of the botched German security response would no doubt have been aired as a consequence of any trial of those involved. Needless to say, denials were immediate and furious, and the producer of the documentary was heavily criticized.

As for the selection of targets, one of the first and most obvious was the kingpin of Palestinian resistance, Arafat, who had been in Israel's crosshairs in one form or another since his emergence at the top of the Palestinian leadership. However, in 1972, he had become too much of an international figure and a cultural icon, and his assassination would certainly have run afoul of Israel's delicate political balance at a time when international sympathy was somewhat in decline.

The first verified assassination attributable to Operation Wrath of God was the killing of Wael Zwaiter, the PLO's Italian representative. Committee X gave the green light for his assassination, and it was carried out on October 16, 1972, a little over a month after the Munich Massacre.

www.ingramcontent.com/pod-product-compliance
Lightning Source LLC
Chambersburg PA
CBHW050406120526
44590CB00015B/1853